In Search of Reality

From Religion to Relationship

Greg Dahl

Copyright © 2024

All Rights Reserved

Disclaimer

I, Greg Dahl, am not a psychologist, therapist, or licensed practitioner. The experiences and insights shared in this book, "In Search of Reality," are based on my personal journey and spiritual encounters with the Holy Spirit, who has been my mentor and guide.

While I believe in the transformative power of these experiences, I do claim that they are universally applicable. God's Word will never fail.

The views and opinions expressed in this book are solely mine and heavily rooted in the Word of God. I share my story in the hope that it may inspire and encourage others on their own spiritual journey.

Readers are encouraged to approach the content of this book with an open mind and heart, consider how these insights may resonate with their own experiences, and let you know that with God, all things are possible. He is my hope and peace in this trying world.

Dedication

To my beloved wife, Theresa!

Words cannot express the depth of my gratitude for you. You are not just my wife but my soulmate, my partner, and my best friend. Your love, support, and unwavering faith have been a constant source of strength and inspiration to me.

You were the first person through whom I truly saw Jesus. Your compassion, kindness, and selflessness reflect His love in ways that continue to amaze me. Your presence in my life is a gift I cherish every day.

I dedicate this book to you, Theresa, as a testament to the profound impact you have had on my life. I promise to love and serve you with my whole heart, now and always. Thank you for being my rock, my light, and my love.

With all my heart,

Greg

Proverbs 31:10-12

A wife of noble character who can find?

She is worth far more than rubies.

Her husband has full confidence in

her and lacks nothing of value.

She brings him good, not harm,

all the days of her life.

Acknowledgments

I am deeply grateful to all those who have supported and encouraged me on my journey of seeking God and understanding reality. Your patience, wisdom, and kindness have been invaluable to me, and I am truly blessed to have you in my life.

While I cannot possibly list everyone who has touched my life in this way, please know that your influence has not gone unnoticed or unappreciated. Each of you has played a significant role in shaping my understanding and guiding me on my path.

Family, friends, mentors, and fellow seekers: thank you for your unwavering support, for listening to my questions and doubts, and for sharing your own insights and experiences with me. You have enriched my life in countless ways, and I am grateful for each of you.

May we continue to journey together, seeking truth, understanding, and God's presence in our lives.

Thank you.

About the Author

Greg is an artist and musician with a pastoral heart whose journey of discovering God and deepening his faith lies at the heart of his life. As a devoted follower of Christ, Greg seeks the Kingdom of God first, which is evident in his everyday life. With a background in Christian songwriting, his creative work includes the album "*The Hand of God,*" as well as various singles.

As a committed leader in his home church, Greg serves as an elder, worship leader, and homegroup overseer, playing a pivotal role in nurturing spiritual growth and community.

Greg's experiences leading worship and seeking God's presence have profoundly shaped his understanding of freedom and reality. His journey from spiritual bondage to freedom underscores his belief in the transformative power of faith and community.

In "*In Search of Reality,*" Greg offers a blend of personal reflection, spiritual insight, and practical guidance. He draws from his own experiences of becoming a New Creation, as described in John 3:3, and personal encounters with the Holy Spirit. His work encourages readers to embark on their own quests for truth found in Christ alone, embracing the challenges and profound rewards of seeking a deeper understanding of reality.

His first book, "In Search of Reality," is complemented by upcoming releases, "Man to Man" and "Father to Father."

Always and Forever,

Theresa

Preface

Contemplating my life's bittersweet journey, I am compelled to acknowledge the myriad experiences that molded me and ultimately guided me toward the redemptive knowledge of Jesus. This book unfolds as a comparison between the depravity of my sin and God's boundless grace and timely yet triumphant intervention in the midst of my struggle with addiction. My earnest prayer is that, as you navigate the pages of my narrative, it serves as an inspiring chronicle that, by the grace of God, empowers you to find freedom.

I show the difference between striving and working your way to heaven versus His grace and mercy. The contrast couldn't be greater than the distance between East and West, as the Bible says.

The scripture from Matthew 5:6 resonates profoundly throughout the pages, encapsulating the essence of my journey and the transformative power of seeking righteousness. It is a promise that those who earnestly hunger and thirst for righteousness will, indeed, be filled.

May this recounting of my personal odyssey and God's Word become a source of encouragement for you, a beacon of hope that God's grace can penetrate the darkest corners of our lives and lead us to victory. As you embark on this journey through my story, may you find solace, inspiration, and, ultimately, the freedom that comes through the redeeming grace of Jesus Christ.

Let me share with you the hope that I have found. My hope is in none other than Jesus Christ, who became my Savior, Lord, and friend at age 30, even though I was a worship leader, leading people to Christ before this time. With the power of the Holy Spirit, I not only did away with my old nature but also utterly killed it, and it helped me emerge as a new creation—a creation that was in Him and brought me to the place where He longs for me to be.

As you're aware, there are various addictions that people struggle with. Some turn to drugs, some to the pursuit of wealth, some to pornography, and others to various pursuits—we can fill in the blank with our personal addictions. All these addictions divert us from our true purpose as someone created for worship. Inescapably, we all worship something or someone; it's an inherent aspect of our creation. Worship fosters intimacy with its object, consuming our thoughts and energies.

God the Father designed us to worship Him alone out of His deep love for His creation, yearning to be in communion with us. This profound connection is evident in tearing the veil in the temple from top to bottom when Jesus sacrificed Himself for us to open Earth up to Heaven.

What we worship becomes our god. That is why God says, "Thou shalt have no other gods before me." He only desires the true intimacy that worship brings.

God the Father loves addicts! He knows that if we receive his gift of salvation and become His disciples, we will become His greatest worshipers because we already know how to worship with our whole hearts.

Join me and my story about breaking off all false gods (addictions). Your freedom in Christ awaits!

If the first chapters of this book become too dark and daunting, skip to chapter 8, where all the good news unfolds. I know that recounting my old life can be depressing at times, but if you find yourself losing attention, please skip to Chapter 8.

Here is a song that I wrote asking the question, "Is Jesus alive and well in you?" Listen to it on YouTube, and let me know what you think. Take your phone out and scan the QR code.

Is Jesus Alive And Well In You

Contents

Chapter 1: In the Beginning

I want to invite you to embark on a spiritual journey with me. The destination is where the Holy Spirit led me into true marital fulfillment through the vows that I made on my wedding day. I will tell you of my deliverance from sexual perversion through pornographic addiction, babysitter's sexual abuse, and true freedom in purity, found only in Jesus, God's Christ.

I will begin with an introduction to the remarkable individuals who helped shape my formative years and my family.

My older brother David, born in Newfoundland, possessed an innate engineering talent. Despite never formally studying it, he could comprehend and build anything, from boats to cars. His dream was always to be a Kodiak Alaska commercial fisherman, a passion he still pursues, even as the industry's toll reflects on his body. David remains an excellent skipper, a mastermind capable of overcoming any challenge.

Dianna, the middle child born in New Orleans, was an incredible artist. Her ability to capture the essence of animals or people in painting or sculpture, even dabbling in stained glass, left me in awe. I believe her artistic talent was indeed a gift.

Born in New Orleans as well, I was the youngest of my siblings. My mom used to introduce me as "the baby of the family." If she were still alive, she would likely call me the family's baby.

My work history is dotted with inconsistencies and fluctuations. At age 12, in more detail, I started bagging groceries for tips on Metlakatla, a small village on the island of Anet in the southeastern panhandle of Alaska, where my father was stationed in the Coast Guard for one and a half years. From 17 to 23, I worked as a commercial fisherman. Actually, I initially worked as a deckhand or skiff operator and eventually became the skipper. During the off-season, I took on various roles, from welding to operating heavy machinery, doing carpentry, pitching sales, and even working as a security guard for a brief period. After leaving the field of commercial fishing, I ventured into opening a business of my own. Named Alascape, it was an anchorage-based landscape company with up to 26 employees. Despite these business pursuits, I couldn't shake the feeling that a relationship with God was desperately missing from my life, even though I never doubted there was a God and that He created everything. 'Do you love me?' 'Can I know you and be your friend?' These were the questions running through my mind from an early age.

Our upbringing primarily unfolded on Kodiak Island, nestled on the northwest side of the Gulf of

Alaska. Gifted with an adventure-filled life, I went fishing, camping, hiking, ridge riding on a snowmobile on a moonlit night, and riding a motorcycle on World War II trails on the island. We would occasionally find an old World War II concrete bunker to explore. Before Kodiak, my dad, who was on a Coast Guard assignment, was stationed in North Carolina and was transferred to Kodiak, Alaska, in 1968. That move led to almost a 4600-mile driving adventure filled with exciting challenges, thrills, and lots of fun. My dad loaded us all into a brand-new Ford truck with a camper and traveled across the United States to Kodiak Island. It was a drive that led us across the US, up through Canada to Seward, Alaska, where we drove onto a ferry called the Tustumena on the way to our final destination, Kodiak Island, where the Coast Guard base was located. The families of my mom and dad thought we were crazy. We owned boats, nice cars, motorcycles, three-wheelers, and snowmobiles—a seemingly average middle-class American family.

My father, Bjorn Dahl, joined the Coast Guard at just 17 years of age and served in the military for twenty-four years. His parents had to sign off a waiver of sorts to give him permission to join the military at that young age. He had a disciplined and strict personality and was a natural-born leader and avid outdoorsman. My grandfather, Bjorn Margido Winter (pronounced Vintor) Dahl, a WWII merchant marine, instilled a love for adventure in my dad. My grandfather immigrated from Norway. My dad said that when my grandfather landed in the United States, he jumped from the ship, found my grandmother, married, and continued his life as a merchant marine. As grandkids, we used to wait for Dad to come home because he would bring us coins from all over the world collected from the ports he had been to.

Despite dropping out of school in the eighth grade, my father loved reading, a trait that fascinated me from an early age. However, owing to my learning disability, I struggled to comprehend written text.

My mother, Rosemary, was born and grew up with her four sisters in New Orleans, just ten blocks from Bourbon Street (a famous street in New Orleans). Her father, Nick Terranova, immigrated from Italy. I remember him telling me the story of his young adulthood. He operated a block ice business with a horse and carriage.

He would have his route to deliver 75-pound ice blocks to his clients. He once said, "Gregory, the refrigerator put me out of business (in his gruff, raspy Italian voice). One by one, my clients would buy that contraption, so I had to get a job in the brewery. I never came home drunk, but I sure came home happy." In his later years, he was as wide as he was tall.

Mom was a devoted housewife with a divine talent for cooking. Spending hours in the kitchen, she crafted culinary masterpieces—stuffed manicotti, bouchons, muffuletta sandwiches, and more. I fully appreciated the magic she worked in the kitchen only after her passing. Her joyful spirit, accompanied by the nostalgic musical tunes of the 1950s and 60s, often led to impromptu dances in the living room. She would hear a good song and say, "Come on, Gregory, let's dance." She would grab my hands, dance, and laugh around the living room. It was the best of times when that happened.

Retaining strong Italian ties from her parents, who immigrated to the US from Italy, she infused our lives with holiday traditions. From milk and cookies for Santa Claus to bunny prints on Easter and painted faces for Halloween, she embraced motherhood with her whole heart.

Despite appearances, we were a family navigating life without the knowledge of God in the Bible. Little did we know that God was calling the Dahl family from the beginning, guiding us toward a collision course with the divine. Our journey to knowing God began through Catholicism, a path chosen by my dad. Sunday Mass, confirmations, and my brother and I serving as altar boys filled our early years.

Challenges marked our upbringing, too. My parents often disagreed, leading to heated arguments that shaped my life perception. Despite their love for us, pride overshadowed humility in their relationship.

When I was six or so, my mother made a seemingly innocent revelation when she shared that my conception was an accident. She cried when she found out she was pregnant with me. I was the third in a row: 3 babies in 3 years. My dad, in marked contrast, wanted to have 11 boys to make his own football team. Despite this, she swiftly reassured me, "But I love you very much." Unfortunately, what resonated within me was the belief that I was a mistake. In the grand tapestry of existence, I navigated between a benevolent God who cares deeply for me and an adversary, Satan, who seeks to kill, steal, and destroy (John 10:10). In that pivotal moment, Satan seized something precious—my sense of value and self-worth. I know I was a mistake to my mother, but what about God? Was I a mistake to Him as well? There had to be a reason why He created me.

The aftermath led me to ponder profound questions. If tragedy befell my family, would I shed a tear for my parents and siblings? Strangely, my answer leaned toward a detached "No." This triggered an internal inquiry: "What is wrong with me? Am I broken?" It's important to note that these feelings weren't solely born from that revelation with my mother; they became a complex web, weaving a narrative where the true essence of love eluded me.

Over the years, that single statement echoed relentlessly in my mind, spanning decades like a persistent, haunting refrain. It became one of the many arrows Satan aimed at me, injecting a toxic thought process: I have no value, I am stupid, a dummy, and utterly worthless. This mental barrage left me in a place of profound darkness, where the concepts of love, joy, and peace seemed elusive. Struggling to find these virtues in my parents, I recognized an unmet yearning within me.

I desired the trait of knowing how to love, an element absent from my immediate surroundings. While I sensed that God held the key to these desires, I remained clueless about the path to attaining them. Paradoxically, even in the depths of my own failings, God was orchestrating a plan, laying the groundwork for His grace and mercy to illuminate my life eventually.

Growing up, my parents frequently engaged in heated arguments, leaving a lasting negative impact on me as a child. The clash of views, distracting factors, and verbal threats painted a tumultuous picture of their relationship. Despite harboring thoughts that they might have married the wrong person, they held on, anchored by the biblical principle, "What God has joined together, let no man separate." Matthew 19:9

I am not sure of my age, but we were visiting grandparents in New Orleans. My mother and dad were in the backyard, and I was on the swing nearby. They were having a heated argument, and all of a sudden, dad pushed my mother to the ground. I jumped off the swing, ready to take my dad out, saying, 'No one touches my mom like that.' Later, my dad came to me and said, "Always protect your mom. No one should do anything like that to her." My dad stepped over that line, and he knew it. I never saw him showing such villainous behavior again.

As a child in Kodiak, I overheard unsettling conversations that shook me morally, instilling a deep sense of fear. The things that I would hear my mother and father say to each other were vicious. I heard accusations that I did not know how to process at the time. I witnessed name-calling and unforgiveness. I didn't see them resolve arguments in a good way. The constant arguing became unbearable. At the tender age of 8, I took it upon myself to intervene. I sat my mom and dad on the couch, attempting to counsel them. I vividly recall my mother's response, "Maybe it takes bringing us down to a childlike level to see our ways." Their commitment to improving their marriage extended to attending 'Marriage Encounters,' a retreat for struggling couples. In an effort to work on their relationship, they even made the difficult decision to place us in foster care for a month, confirming my negative thoughts of who I was: Unwanted, a mistake. Despite the challenges, my parents' determination to navigate the complexities of marriage reflected a profound commitment to our family's well-being. They were better after going through 'Marriage Encounters' for a while, but arguing started once again, and we were in the same place of discord. One thing I saw was that my parents would stay together until my mother graduated into heaven.

Just a side note: The last year of my mother's life was the most joyful for both of them. She forgave, and true joy flooded their relationship. My dad served her like a queen at her bedside. My mother realized how futile unforgiveness was, and my dad became humble. This was beautiful!

However, every special occasion, from Christmas to Easter and even Mother's Day, carried a shadow of tension as it inevitably spiraled into another argument between my parents. The echoes of their discord became the soundtrack to our holidays. Tragically, we, the children, absorbed this pattern of conflict, learning to argue much like our parents did. Joyous celebrations should have morphed into moments tainted by their noisy arguments and raucous altercations. The anger that brewed within us turned festive occasions into opportunities for turmoil, creating a stark contrast to the joy that these days should have held. From my perspective, surprisingly, my sister managed to navigate through this turbulent atmosphere with a resilience that set her apart from the rest of us.

Mirroring the pattern set by our parents, my brother David and I found ourselves entangled in arguments, grappling with conflicts without a clear understanding of resolution. This constant friction hindered the development of a strong bond between us—a connection improved for the better later in life after receiving Jesus as our Lord and Savior. There was pent-up anger in both David and me. On one occasion, when we were arguing, I pulled a butter knife on him, and on another occasion, I was in his garden and would not get out. He was on the porch with the shovel just after turning up the soil. I loved the feeling of the soft dirt between my toes. David threw the shovel at me, and the blade hit my big toe. I remember it hanging by a thread, but I am sure it wasn't that bad looking back on the incident. It was just a cut on my toe, and Mom bandaged me up.

While I recognize that my parents did their best, I couldn't escape the disdain I harbored for the persistent discord that dominated our household. The aversion to their arguments became a common sentiment with me; after all, no child wishes to witness their parents trapped in a perpetual cycle of disagreement.

In the subsequent years, around 1982, my father underwent a transformative experience, embracing salvation that only Jesus can provide. During this period, he candidly revealed his past struggles with alcohol addiction, shedding light on a facet of his life that had contributed to the tumultuous arguments with my mother. Surprisingly, I had never witnessed this side of him, unaware of the battles he faced with alcohol.

Despite their efforts to shield us from emotional turmoil, I observed my parents grappling with stress, striving to maintain a facade of happiness and strength for the sake of our family. However, beneath the surface, our family unit was gradually unraveling, mirroring the strains caused by my father's past struggles with alcoholism and my mother's unforgiveness.

My mother and dad separated for a while, and mom and the kids moved to Juneau, Alaska, where we restarted our lives. Mom worked as a janitor at the Capital building. I guess she started to date because one night, I heard some noise coming from the living room and caught my mom with another guy. I quickly turned around and went back to my room, with my mom following to explain. Again, confusion sunk deeper into me. My foundation was shaking again.

While we were still living in Juneau with my parents, who were still separated one day, I spotted a church and strongly desired to talk with God while walking home from school. Approaching the imposing double doors, I pulled them, only to find them locked. At that moment, a disheartening thought crossed my mind: "I guess I can't talk to God. God is not supposed to be closed". But He was for me. I couldn't ask Him the question that lingered in my mind: "Was I a mistake?" This experience planted a seed of false belief—I came to view the doors to God as forever closed for me, reinforcing the idea that, being a mistake, I was unworthy of talking to God.

This skewed perspective lingered until age 30, suggesting that God had cast me out, shutting off the doors to heaven for me. Despite this, an unyielding determination to seek God persisted within me. It led me onto a religious path, convinced that if I could only be good enough, generous enough, or immersed enough in His Word, I might earn His acknowledgment and, perhaps, His love. Throughout adolescence and into adulthood, I grappled with the belief that I was unlovable, propelling me to jump through religious hoops in a desperate quest for God's affection and the approval of those around me. I would ask myself, "Who could love someone like me?" So, unwittingly, I manipulated those around me to gain their affection.

I found myself trapped in continued self-pity, which I humorously dubbed the "Eeyore syndrome," drawing inspiration from the Winnie the Pooh cartoon. In moments when I yearned for someone's affection, I would adopt a demeanor of melancholy. Without revealing the source of my distress, I sought solace in the attention that ensued. Reflecting on it now, it seems rather disheartening—a poignant testament to my desperation for connection, resorting to manipulating people into befriending me through a facade of depression. I smiled a lot, but only to hide my brokenness inside.

Another childhood memory on Kodiak Island was that at age 5 or 6, I was sexually abused by my babysitter. I will not be graphic, but when she was violating me, she would demand affirmation, "Do you love me?" and I would reply, "Yes, I love everyone in the whole wide world." I remember her asking me that many times. And that was my reply. I had no clue or understanding what was happening to me. I now know these assaults on my youthful innocence and purity opened the door to the demonic in my life—ultimately into a life spiraling into pornography. Looking back on this one-time incident, I see my innocence and love for the world and its people—a God-infused trait.

Growing up, the constant feeling of falling short in my father's eyes haunted me. "Hold that nail straight. Hold that board higher. You could have done it better. Why won't you do what I say?" The disappointment I believed I was to my dad rang in my mind, fueling a belief that I was inherently unintelligent and destined for failure.

I even thought of an invention for a drill that, if it had a level bubble on the top, I could hold the drill straight and wouldn't hear my dad say in a yelling, frustrated voice, "Hold it straight." As he grabbed the drill to make it plumb, I would focus on the bubble if it were there. It would stop me from being a mess-up in my dad's eyes, and then he would love me.

Academic struggles only added weight to this self-fulfilling prophecy, a prophecy later compounded by the revelation of my ADHD (Attention Deficit Hyperactivity Disorder). I was hyper, couldn't focus on anything for very long, and in present-day language, it is "Squirrel."

The lie that I was a mistake, unwanted by my mother, and unpleasing to my father echoed the devil's deceptive narrative. These falsehoods were my stepping stones to bondage and misery. However, God, who is greater, later freed me with a grand unveiling of His purpose in my life. I have learned and know that to the core of my being, I never quit the pursuit of God, for He was and is constantly pursuing me!

Indeed, my journey paints the picture of a troubled child navigating the complexities of growing up. However, amid the formidable challenges, I've come to understand that everyone faces their own trials and tribulations, with varying degrees of difficulty.

The unyielding pursuit of my heart by my Heavenly Father remains unwavering. His love, unparalleled and infinite, seeks to fulfill my life in ways the world cannot. In my struggle, He stands as the ultimate source of solace and purpose, ready to guide me toward a life enriched with His divine presence.

The journey of life is filled with numerous distractions that can lead me astray from God's carefully crafted divine plan. It's a constant battle between God's purpose for my life and Satan's deceptive schemes furtively aimed at derailing me from the path of righteousness.

However, amid this cosmic struggle, God's overarching plan is to soften my heart, allowing Him to mold me into a masterpiece He had in mind from the beginning. Even my challenges and hardships were transformed into tools for His artistic hand. Through the unveiling of my own story, I pray that His heart, overflowing with love and grace, becomes apparent to you who embark on the journey of my experiences. May it serve as a witness to the transformative power of God's redemptive work in our lives. Amen!

Chapter 2: Junior High, Highschool, and Beyond

Navigating through childhood is inherently challenging, particularly being raised in a tumultuous family setting. The impact of such an upbringing had adverse effects on my personal development. Yet, what was intended for harm by Satan, God orchestrated for good. Throughout my recollection, embracing who God made me be was a formidable task, but amidst the struggles, I consistently sensed the divine pull of God.

In the 8th grade on Kodiak Island, I had a summer job washing cars at a small car dealership. This is where I was first exposed to pornography, an unfortunate moment where Satan seized and distorted a God-given ability in me, and that was my ability to dream and see pictures in my mind that were supposed to be used for the Kingdom of God. As "the adversary comes to kill, steal, and destroy, but Jesus came to give me life and more abundant." (John 10:10), Satan stole from me again. I was an addict at first sight. What I see has the ability to sear in my mind and take over my thoughts. This addiction lasted until age 30.

In my school years, specific memories stand out and are worth recounting. The early stages of my academic journey, extending up to junior high, were marked by considerable struggles, exacerbated by the challenges of ADHD and dyslexia, conditions not widely understood at the time. One vivid recollection from high school involves a teacher publicly mocking me in class for misspelling "girl" as "gril." The incident occurred during an assignment where we were asked to write about recent experiences. In my attempt at humor, I wrote, "I was walking down the hallway following a foxy gril." The teacher proceeded to read it aloud to the entire class, leading to humiliation as laughter ensued, reinforcing the negative beliefs ingrained in my mindset. These instances, I now recognize, were the brutal workings of Satan, employing various tactics to anchor me in false beliefs.

Due to my diminished self-esteem and the challenges posed by ADHD, I struggled to develop proficient reading skills during my academic journey, graduating from high school with a reading level like that of a third grader. Reading aloud in class became daunting, triggering nervousness and occasional stuttering. I concentrated intensely on pronouncing individual words, which caused me to forget the ones before, resulting in a lack of understanding. As a coping mechanism, I eventually resorted to cheating on tests and enlisting others to complete my homework, unwittingly exacerbating the problem.

To this day, the challenge of reading persists despite my roles as an author and songwriter, even extending to tasks like drafting contracts and crafting short stories. Reflecting on this, it's awe-inspiring to consider the grace bestowed upon me by God. I've come to understand that ADHD is not a learning disability but, rather, a gift from God. Scriptures like Jeremiah 1:5,

"I knew you before you were born," and Psalm 139:13-14, "You knit me together in my mother's womb. You are fearfully and wonderfully made," reinforce the notion that God doesn't make mistakes, contrary to my belief at the time. ADHD, when submitted to God's authority, transforms into the original gift that He created. My imagination flourishes, allowing me to perceive perspectives that only God could provide. Regularly dreaming, I encounter God, while ADHD emerges as a unique and valuable gift for the Kingdom of God. Let me share one of my dreams with you, and you tell me if my head in the clouds is used by God.

Let me set the stage for you: I was about 32 years old after becoming a new creation, which I will talk about in chapter 9 of this book. It was two years after becoming born again. I had fallen back into my old sin of pornography after being free from it for two years. I was devastated, to say the least. And as I failed my Father, I want to distance myself from Him because of my shame. But I didn't; I ran to Him, and He gave me a gift. I went up to the church where I would spend every morning with Him in worship. I had an open vision.

This is what I call it when I am falling awake but captured in this vision as a participant created by God.

The scene was an old Western slave auction platform. We (the slaves) were down below, where the buyers were looking at the goods (us). I was in the midline, with my head hung low, as all the slaves were.

I saw this man dressed in black with gold rings and necklaces. He obviously had money, but there was something about him that I did not like, so I remember thinking, "I don't want to be bought by him." I knew he would be a bad taskmaster. One by one, buyers were checking us out, each one with the same conclusion in my mind. Then I saw a plainly dressed man, neat and modest. I noticed him taking his pointer finger and lifting the chin of each slave to look into their eyes. I watched and saw a little smile on each slave for a brief moment. But even before he got to me, I was convinced he was the one.

He finally got to me and lifted my chin. It is hard to describe the feeling that went through my spirit when we locked eyes, but a flood of love, joy, and peace shot through my soul.

Oh, if I could only be bought by him. I know he would be a good master. I would serve him for the rest of my life. I could devote myself to him and give him all that I have. But it looked like he did not have much money. Surely, he couldn't buy all of us.

The auction started, and people were bought and sold. My turn arrived. I could not see the man. I frantically scanned the crowd, but he was nowhere to be seen. The price was getting higher and higher, with a sense of despair sweeping over me. Besides, I thought he didn't have enough money to buy me. As the auctioneer was saying, "going once, going twice," my heart sank, then the man that I longed to be bought by levitated above the crowd, and nail scars appeared on his hands and feet, and a piercing appeared on his side. At that time, I heard the auctioneer say, "SOLD TO THE HIGHEST BIDDER," and he bought me! After the auctioneer's final words, I snapped out of the vision.

Flooded with tears, I again realized his love. He brought me into freedom! Just when I needed Him, he came through. This is my amazing God who gives grace.

Let's come back to the narrative.

Academic challenges often resulted in failures, prompting me to compensate as best I could. To accommodate the difficulties, I found solace in pretending, concealing my genuine struggles.

In junior high, I raced motocross. I never got a first-place trophy, but dozens of second-place trophies lined my chest of drawers in my room. Even a second-place win made me a failure in my mind.

Despite these hurdles, athletics emerged as a strength. While basketball was my primary joy, I also participated in track and cross-country, channeling my passion into sports. I quickly rose to Varsity on every Kodiak high school team. In my senior year, we were 22 and 2 for the basketball season. I loved the recognition that sports gave. All the accolades became another addiction, performing for people for the praise. The roar of the crowd when I made a basket was exhilarating.

During my teenage years, a memorable moment unfolded during my transition from Catholicism to Christianity. My friends, who were Christians, radiated happiness in their lives, displaying an unwavering faith in God through Jesus. Honestly, I admired their faith and desired that connection with the Lord for myself. I wanted to fit in. They encouraged me to embrace Christianity, assuring me that by inviting Jesus into my life and believing in His sacrifice on the cross for my sins, I could find joy and belonging among this community of believers and be changed forever. Intrigued, I wholeheartedly embraced their advice, inviting Jesus into my heart that night. However, the experience didn't unfold as anticipated. There were no fireworks, angelic melodies, or power to overcome my sins. I was still stuck in my addictions. Yet, skilled at maintaining a façade, I continued to wear a smile while grappling with internal brokenness, trapped in my struggles with sin.

Despite my efforts, my pain persisted, and it became disheartening to witness others in church seemingly complete with faith and joy. I struggled with a sense of inadequacy, feeling like I wasn't doing enough to please God. I thought that if I worked harder, He might look my way. This feeling of falling short led my faith to waver, and the more I strived, the more distant I felt in His eyes.

However, giving up wasn't an option for me, as I held onto the belief that "He is the way, the truth, and the life, and no one comes to the Father except through Him" (John 14:6). Even with a solid foundation of Biblical teachings, I still had that void, a gaping hole in my understanding of Him, desiring more knowledge and a deeper connection.

At 19, I thought joining the military would solve my problems of being a scatterbrain, aspiring to become a Navy Seal. However, I encountered an unexpected hurdle during the written test, particularly in mathematics. The irony of struggling with math, rather than the challenges associated with reading, struck me. I attempted to retake the math test in the presence of a fellow candidate engaging in blatant cheating, diverting my attention from the task at hand. Amidst these circumstances, marked by ADHD, I failed to pass the test, intensifying the profound sense of failure that loomed over me. The weight of this experience proved overwhelming, amplifying the belief that I was destined for insignificance.

Nevertheless, a burning pursuit continued to stir within. "I want to know You, God." I would attend church and be involved as much as possible, thinking I would get God to love me. I would pray, "Look at me! Look this way, God!"

Yet, amid these religious practices, a profound void persisted—a notable absence that left me on edge. This void compelled me to contemplate His presence and significance continually, along with my depraved mind that was now captured by pornography, and I was always trying to look good on the outside to hide my pain. Engulfed in an ongoing struggle, I sought tirelessly to earn His love and acceptance. Delving into His word, I discovered accounts of Him communicating with people, and an intense desire arose within me to be counted among those who experienced such divine interaction.

I was reading the Book of Job, and in chapter 26, I found a beautifully articulated, awe-inspiring description of God's nature. It vividly portrays His majesty and creative prowess, showcasing His divine acts.

He stretches out the northern skies across the vast emptiness, suspending the earth with unparalleled grace. The waters, encapsulated in His clouds, remain weightless, proof of His delicate balance in creation.

Even the full moon finds itself veiled by His clouds, while the horizon becomes a distinct boundary between light and darkness.

The heavens themselves tremble at His mere rebuke, illustrating the immense power He wields. He stirs the seas with unparalleled might, and with profound wisdom, He dissects Rahab. His breath alone transforms the skies into a canvas of beauty, and His hand masterfully pierces the gliding serpent. These descriptions, however, are but the outer fringe of His vast works, leaving us to ponder the subtle whispers of His greatness. As we marvel at these wonders, the thunder of His power remains a mystery beyond our comprehension.

Doesn't the description in Job 26 just evoke a sense of majesty? It resonates with truth – God is truly MAJESTIC!

Observing others who walked closely with the Lord, immersed in His love, I realized that God loved them dearly. Motivated by this, I continued my pursuit, delving into learning and participating in Bible studies.

In my early twenties in 1984, I even enrolled in one year of Bible College called St. Paul Bible College outside Minneapolis, Crown College, and two years of Bible school at Abbott Loop Community Church that Theresa and I attended. Despite the extensive teachings, there was a persistent feeling that I hadn't truly known God. I could see Him in others but not me. I was too tainted. It seemed I knew only about Him, but I didn't have the intimate connection I longed for. Questions arose: Was I less faithful, did I not do enough, or did I pray enough? Oh, that's right, I made a mistake. Regardless, the more I sought God, the more it seemed like the doors to my relationship with Him were locked, leading me deeper into the struggle with pornography and a performance mentality. This internal conflict highlighted the hypocrisy in my life.

I embarked on paths and encountered circumstances that eventually shaped my faith. Throughout most of my life, I ran in desperation to seek Him while wrestling with the growing presence of sin. As sin grew, my desire to know Him grew as well. The conflict between sin and seeking Him became the war in my life of desperation.

Religion became an all-encompassing force in my life, and I tirelessly jumped through every hoop it presented, such as praying, serving, and giving. Each attempt ended in a disheartening failure to get God's attention. Whenever I gave or served, I would look up to heaven and ask, "Is this good enough? Can you love me now?" Religion gave rise to frustration in me.

Little did I know, this was all part of God's plan, setting the stage for a revelation that would transform my life. He was letting me get to my bottom.

Allow me to offer you a definition of "Religion": It involves humans attempting to reach God through their efforts. However, God desires us to come to the cross of Jesus and believe that act took away all our sins and strivings. His ways are not ours, and He has the way to the Father. He longs to be both our Lord and friend. Believing that we can earn our way to God is akin to trying to manipulate Him. This approach is futile and fails to bring the peace of knowing Him. God may let us persist in religious striving until we recognize that it is not through our works but by His grace that we come to Him (Ephesians 2:8-9).

There is a story in the Bible that is shared about a tumultuous upbringing in Genesis where Joseph was sold into slavery due to jealousy of his older brothers. As he eventually rose to power to save all of them, God likewise had a plan for all of us to get out of slavery.

Let's pick up the story starting in Genesis 50:14 (NIV), where God raised Joseph into power to save his family:

14. After burying his father, Joseph returned to Egypt, together with his brothers and all the others who had gone with him to bury his father.

15. When Joseph's brothers saw that their father was dead, they said, "What if Joseph holds a grudge against us and pays us back for all the wrongs we did to him?"

16. So they sent word to Joseph, saying, "Your father left these instructions before he died."

17. "This is what you are to say to Joseph: I ask you to forgive your brothers the sins and the wrongs they committed in treating you so badly. Now please forgive the sins of the servants of the God of your father." When their message came to him, Joseph wept.

18. His brothers then came and threw themselves down before him. "We are your slaves," they said.

19. But Joseph said to them, "Don't be afraid. Am I in the place of God?"

20. *You intended to harm me, but God intended it for good to accomplish what is now being done, the saving of many lives.*

21. So then, don't be afraid. I will provide for you and your children." And he reassured them and spoke kindly to them.

God will make a way because He is in the pursuit of my heart! Throughout my life, I have had opportunities to meet God, but for some reason, I turn the other way. What Satan intends for bad, God will turn for good. I am sure that there were times when Joseph was discouraged, but after seeing the work that the Lord wanted to accomplish through him, he had the understanding and willingness to forgive and see what God was doing through him. Joseph embraced his destiny.

Chapter 3: Devastation

James 1:13-15 warns against attributing temptation to God, emphasizing that temptation arises from one's desires, leading to sin and, ultimately, death. Reflecting on my experience, addiction seized me mercilessly, and explicit images became indelibly etched in my mind, leaving me powerless to resist. The initial allure of a woman's body marked the beginning of a rapid descent into addiction, orchestrated by Satan with precise timing. Each glance fueled the addiction, trapping me in an inescapable loop, spiraling downward.

Given my self-perception, the swift entanglement is not surprising. Satan exploited my vulnerabilities, offering an apparent escape from reality, and I fully embraced it. In those moments, all my faults and failures felt momentarily concealed. However, as the addiction tightened its grip, my mind became consumed by lustful thoughts. These thoughts infiltrated every aspect of my daily and dream life, disrupting my focus on anything else. My mental landscape became cluttered, and my dreams were held captive, having the ability to control them. In my dreams, I could willingly do whatever I wanted with women, and it got worse and worse in my dreams, and during the day, I could imagine the same.

Efforts to suppress these thoughts proved futile as they grew stronger, thriving on my vulnerability and insecurities. I would ask the Lord to take them away to no avail. The internal struggle persisted, torn between the desire to break free from this addiction and the fleeting pleasure it provided. Who can save me from this wretched sin?

Despite my attempts to seek God for solace, the grip of addiction tightened, fostering guilt and shame, perpetuating a distressing cycle. Trapped in this struggle, my relationships with others suffered, creating a disconnect and living a double life. In this dark period, Satan's insidious plan extended beyond addiction, influencing my beliefs about how women should be treated and reducing them to commodities for consumption devoid of the reverence they deserved.

Reflecting on these distressing memories, a pause is necessary to interject some uplifting scripture.

"For I know the plans I have for you," declares the LORD, "plans to prosper you and not to harm you, plans to give you hope and a future."

–Jeremiah 29:11

"For God so loved the world that he gave his one and only Son, that whoever believes in him shall not perish but have eternal life."

–John 3:16

"He does not treat us as our sins deserve or repay us according to our iniquities. For as high as the heavens are above the earth, so great is his love for those who fear him; as far as the east is from the west, so far has he removed our transgressions from us."

-Psalms 103:10-12

These scriptures refresh my soul and bring hope. His living and active words carry such rejuvenation!

Contemplating my journey, I can't ignore the malevolent role Satan played in my addiction battle. It commenced with a seed of curiosity sown during my early teenage years and possibly when my babysitter molested me. Unbeknownst to me, this seemingly innocent curiosity burgeoned into an overwhelming temptation, swiftly steering me down a gloomy and ruinous path.

Amidst my internal conflicts fueled by my false perception of myself, Satan exploited my vulnerabilities, murmuring deceptive assurances of pleasure and satisfaction. He perverted God's splendid design for sexuality, contorting it into a shallow and synthetic substitute that left me hollow and yearning for more of this illusory life.

Satan, the great deceiver, exhibits a shrewd understanding of human nature, including the unique gifts and talents bestowed upon me by God. His strategy involves exploiting my vulnerabilities and weaknesses, transforming them into entry points for manipulation and distortion of my God-given gifts for his malevolent purposes and my sinful nature. He preyed on my fears and past traumas, using them as ammunition to undermine my confidence and hinder the full development of the talents God has given me. In scripture, he is known as the lord of the Flies, targeting our open wounds, symbolized by our traumas.

However, I must remember that God's love and grace surpass any scheme Satan may employ. Through repentance, faith, prayer, and seeking God, He can restore my gifts from Satan's grasp, utilizing them to bring Him glory. Recognizing my worth in God's eyes and relying on His strength, I, through the power of the Holy Spirit, can thwart Satan's schemes and reclaim my gifts for their intended purpose—spreading love, goodness, and light amid darkness. As Joel 2:25 states, "I will repay you for the years the locusts have eaten."

If you haven't already, would you take a moment to ask Jesus to become the Lord of your life? He alone can bring the freedom you desire.

Reflecting on my journey, I can discern the profound impact of the struggle. The constant fear of judgment, rejection, or failure compelled me to go to great lengths to hide who I was. I had to fit in and gain acceptance.

This became a survival strategy—a means to shield myself from the pain of exclusion and the accompanying loneliness. Unfortunately, in my pursuit of becoming a people-pleaser, I unwittingly detached from the identity God had planned for me. I found myself living a life dictated by the expectations of others rather than in alignment with my authentic desires, dreams, and the purpose for which God created me. I didn't know how to say "no!"

Now, I perceive His might in all its glory and beauty. Although my story involves internal devastation, I know it has heightened my appreciation for the fulfillment of experiencing His light. I am now fully engulfed in Him (Luke 7:47). Therefore, I tell you, her many sins have been forgiven, as her great love has shown, but whoever has been forgiven little loves little. I have been forgiven so much.

Chapter 4: Meaningless

Pleasing my family, friends, and God, life started to reach a point where everything felt hollow and meaningless. Amidst sports, partying, having money, and relationships, I attempted to embrace Christianity more fully. In Kodiak High School, I was invited to a Young Life meeting, an organization for both Christian and un-churched kids, where they explained the path to becoming a Christian through faith in Jesus Christ and his accomplishments on the cross and in his resurrection.

The Young Life meetings were weekly. I could hear about God and scope the girls as well. I was feeding my flesh with my girlfriend and hearing about the teachings of Jesus, hoping to draw closer to God and find a sense of direction, even becoming a leader and picking up girls. So twisted! Whenever I sang during these gatherings, people would praise me, saying, "You have a gift." It provided a sense of validation that I enjoyed. Despite this external affirmation, I still felt alone and abandoned. I made numerous friends in church but lacked the courage to share my struggles with anyone.

In an effort to fit in, I prayed the salvation prayer again, but deep down, I doubted that God could truly forgive me. Who could love someone like me? Unfortunately, again, there was no transformative change in my life. Briefly, I refrained from sinful acts, but soon, lustful thoughts overran my mind, and I was consumed once again. I pursued relationships with girls who could provide what I wanted, by the grace of God, they were few. Unbeknownst to me, I was perverting the gifts that God had bestowed upon me once again.

I was aware that God was the way, yet the allure of sin captured me. It clung to me like a magnet, exerting constant pressure on my soul, insisting that it wouldn't release its grip. My flesh, as well, resisted letting go, with a reservoir of sin inside me waiting to burst forth. I succumbed to those desires as much as I could. However, God protected me from acting out much of what was in my mind. Like a carrot dangling in front of a donkey, I continued to chase the pursuit of popularity, the need to belong, and the desire for acceptance from somewhere, mistakenly believing that these things sustained life.

There were no dramatic lights or thunderous changes. My walk remained unchanged. I was still as self-seeking as before; I had merely uttered a prayer. Despite that, I knew deep down that I lacked a genuine relationship with God, the Father.

Here is an artistic writing that I wrote many years ago:

'I' is an inherently selfish person. Should I attempt to escape? But there I find 'Me.' Wherever I venture, there I am. I've endeavored to elude I, yet it outpaces me. 'I' demands a burdensome load beyond my endurance. The demand of I is uncontrollable. Who can rescue 'Me' from the clutches of I? It must be the one who is flawless and mighty. The self-centeredness that 'I' embodies is overwhelming; its incessant demands are unrelenting. I shall resist the pull of I and defy its directives. I will prioritize others, showering them with kindness. I will submit to the One who has the power to kill 'I.'

This gives a glimpse of the war that was raging inside me.

Behind the façade I presented to the world, I was acutely aware of the stark contrast between the persona I projected and the person I became when no one was watching. The inconsistency between my public display of piety and private indulgence haunted me. I had a girlfriend with whom I engaged in inappropriate relations, and despite knowing it was wrong, I continued down that path.

The weight of hypocrisy bore heavily on my conscience, overshadowing any perceived progress. It made me reflect on those hypocrites in the church, and it reminded me of the apostle Paul, who, before meeting Jesus, lived a life steeped in scripture and adherence to the law. Despite his intentions to please God, he ended up persecuting Christians, believing he was doing God's will. His encounter with Jesus on the road to Damascus was a transformative moment. His perspective shifted, his sight was changed, and he was purified in an instant. The scriptures came alive for him, and he realized the gravity of his previous actions. This turning point in Paul's life was a seismic shift, a profound reorientation of beliefs. It serves as a testament to God's mercy, illustrating how one can be dedicated to a certain way of life only to discover, with divine grace, that it was misguided.

I earnestly sought righteousness, I hungered and thirsted, and I eventually was satisfied, as Matthew 5:6 assures. It's just a matter of time. One thing I couldn't let go of was the pursuit of a personal relationship with Jesus.

Drawing inspiration from John 10:27–28 (KJV), "My sheep hear my voice, and I know them, and they follow me: and I give unto them eternal life; and they shall never perish, neither shall any man pluck them out of my hand." This scripture resonated deeply with me, emphasizing the assurance of eternal life for those who follow Christ. However, I did not hear his voice or have the power to overcome my sin. I was aware that I still lacked the genuine connection with God that I desired. I still believed that I was unlovable, a mistake.

I know of a man who grappled with the same struggles as I did. Unable to bear the frustration of living a double life, attending church while battling issues with lust, he grew angry with God and walked away. I believe he was on the verge of his own Road to Damascus experience, but he quit too soon. The message here is clear: never quit, never give up. The Damascus Road moment will come.

Matthew 5:6 *Those who hunger and thirst for righteousness will be filled.*

My Damascus moment didn't unfold until I reached the age of 30. Before delving into that pivotal experience, there's more to share about the journey leading up to that crucial intersection.

Amidst my struggles, stepping into the church became an emotional labyrinth. The sermons, once a source of inspiration, now felt like targeted admonitions aimed solely at me, fortifying my unworthiness. Doubts about my place in that sacred space sank deeper. Paradoxically, within those hallowed walls, I also found moments of solace, like a healing balm to my wounded soul, providing temporary relief. But if I truly knew God, I would have the power to overcome this sin in my life just like Acts

1:8. To "be my witness" means that you will have the power to live in freedom. The power to overcome sin.

The church community presented a dual reality of comfort and unease. Genuine smiles and warmth from fellow brothers and sisters created a profound sense of belonging, a reminder that redemption was within reach. The sermons instilled hope, suggesting that change was possible, and the supportive fellowship assured me I wasn't alone in my struggles. Yet, a persistent fear lingered—that if they knew the real me, they would turn away in disgust. I grappled with the dichotomy between my addiction and the yearning for transformation, amplified by the unspoken stigma that intensified the shame I already carried. I would go up to the front for alter calls weeping, but the weeping was out of self-pity, not a genuine brokenness of disappointing my heavenly Father.

Addiction of any sort brings a person down to his worst unless they are addicted to Jesus. It exposes the rawest aspects of who we are. In my case, my battle with addiction, hypocrisy, and self-worth takes center stage.

As I battled my inner demons (which were truly demonic), I found myself slipping back into the embrace of my old habits time and time again. I questioned myself whether true redemption was possible or if I was destined to remain ensnared in my self-destructive patterns.

I was going through the same thing that Paul was working out in his life. It was most likely not my addiction but the clash between this life and the Kingdom of God.

"For in my inner being, I delight in God's law (23), but I see another law at work in the members of my body, waging war against the law of my mind and making me a prisoner of the law of sin at work within my members."

–Romans 1:21

But let's hang on to this:

"For God is greater than our hearts, and he knows everything."

–John 3:20

I believed that I was lapping up life when, in fact, I was lapping up death. The deceiver is cunning.

"Be self-controlled and alert. Your enemy, the devil, prowls around like a roaring lion looking for someone to devour."

–Peter 5:8

When I do not exercise self-control, I am in jeopardy of being consumed by Satan. Self-control is one of the fruits of the Spirit.

"They must keep hold of the deep truths of the faith with a clear conscience."

–Timothy 3:9

This was my condition before my Damascus experience.

"For although they knew God, they neither glorified him as God nor gave thanks to him, but their thinking became futile, and their foolish hearts were darkened. "

–Romans 7:22

There are three things at play: the devil, my sinful nature, and the Kingdom of God.

The devil can't make me do anything, but he can prey upon me. The demonic is all around me, shooting darts or arrows of deceit at me. Just as the verse in 1 Peter says, "He prowls around looking for someone to devour."

He tries to prey on me; he tempts me, just like Jesus in the desert.

The Temptation of Jesus

Then Jesus was led by the Spirit into the desert to be tempted by the devil. After fasting forty days and forty nights, he was hungry. The tempter came to him and said, "If you are the Son of God, tell these stones to become bread."

Jesus answered, "It is written: 'Man does not live on bread alone, but on every word that comes from the mouth of God. "

Then, the devil took him to the holy city and had him stand on the highest point of the temple. "If you are the Son of God," he said, "throw yourself down. For it is written:

'He will command his angels concerning you, and they will lift you up in their hands so that you will not strike your foot against a stone.'

"Jesus answered him, "It is also written: 'Do not put the Lord your God to the test."

Again, the devil took him to a very high mountain and showed him all the kingdoms of the world and their splendor. "All this I will give you," he said, "if you will bow down and worship me."

Jesus said to him, "Away from me, Satan! For it is written: 'Worship the Lord your God and serve him only."

Then the devil left him, and angels came and attended him."

–Matthew 4:1–11 (NIV)

If Jesus was tempted, I can bet Satan has my number. But I have weapons, as Jesus did in this passage of scripture.

I was created to worship, and I will worship something or someone. It is inevitable. It is my nature to worship. An addiction is worship to that thing. When God said there shall be no other gods before me, addictions are gods before Him that I am worshipping. But if I know him, He gives me armor to live a pure life.

God loves addicts! Yes, that is right. He knew that if I turned from my wicked ways and worshiped him, I would be one of the greatest worshippers.

The Armor of God

"(10) Finally, be strong in the Lord and in his mighty power. (11) Put on the full armor of God so that you can take your stand against the devil's schemes. (12) For our struggle is not against flesh and blood, but against the rulers, against the authorities, against the powers of this dark world, and against the spiritual forces of evil in the heavenly realms. (13) Therefore, put on the full armor of God, so that when the day of evil comes, you may be able to stand your ground, and after you have done everything, to stand. (14) Stand firm then, with the belt of truth buckled around your waist, with the breastplate of righteousness in place, (15) and with your feet fitted with the readiness that comes from the gospel of peace. (16) In addition to all this, take up the shield of faith, with which you can extinguish all the flaming arrows of the evil one. (17) Take the helmet of salvation and the sword of the Spirit, which is the Word of God. (18) And pray in the Spirit on all occasions with all kinds of prayers and requests. With this in mind, be alert and always keep on praying for all the saints."–Eph. 6: 10-18

Understanding the practical application of spiritual principles proved to be the elusive aspect of my quest for God. Despite knowing the scriptures thoroughly, I followed the advice of pastors and well-intentioned individuals: "When tempted, put on the armor. Pray. Declare, 'I am putting on the helmet of salvation; I am putting on the breastplate of righteousness.'" Yet, despite these verbal efforts, I would inevitably fall. The frustration of this cycle may be familiar to you.

At that time, God's Word was not alive in me, but it was on the verge of becoming so. In my religious fervor, I diligently followed instructions, doing what everyone advised, only to find myself falling each time. This repeated failure reinforced a belief that I was worthless, powerless, and every other "less" imaginable and still was closed off to God. In my pursuit of self-worth and satisfaction, I fed the beast within, hindering my ability to belong and receive love. My self-destructive actions became a barrier to the connection I longed for.

"How much more, then, will the blood of Christ, who through the eternal Spirit offered himself unblemished to God, cleanse our consciences from acts that lead to death, [1] so that we may serve the living God!"

-Hebrews 9:14

"Let us draw near to God with a sincere heart in full assurance of faith, having our hearts sprinkled to

cleanse us from a guilty conscience and having our bodies washed with pure water."

–Hebrews 10:22

"Pray for us. We are sure that we have a clear conscience and desire to live honorably in every way."

–Hebrews 13:18

This is what I longed for and knew that I did not have, however,

"those who hunger and thirst after righteousness WILL be filled."

–Matthew 5:6

I must understand what this verse says in Ephesians 6:12 as I read, *"For our struggle is not against flesh and blood, but against the rulers, against the authorities, against the powers of this dark world and against the spiritual forces of evil in the heavenly realms."*

You see, I was not the problem, my friends were not the problem, and the people who failed me were not the problem either. It was the powers of darkness waging war against my soul and my fallen nature.

I had not yet had my second birth, which John talks about in John 3:3 when he was talking to Nicodemus.

Jesus replied, "Very truly I tell you, no one can see the kingdom of God unless they are born again.

Chapter 5: Community College & Bible College

I stood at a crossroads in my life, confronted by the harsh truth that my relentless pursuit of pleasure had ushered me into a realm of emptiness, despair, and living in a dark fantasy life. The allure of parties, popularity, and constant distractions had only provided fleeting relief for the void within me, knowing the need for a significant change.

As I contemplate my community college experience in Coos Bay, Oregon, a twinge of regret accompanies the reflection. The semester I had eagerly enrolled in became overshadowed by the irresistible pull of the party scene. I found myself caught between the demands of academia and the enticements of a wild lifestyle. In the end, my grades suffered, and I was left with merely a fraction of the academic credits I had initially aimed for.

However, the repercussions extended beyond academic setbacks. The hard-earned money from my job as a commercial fisherman swiftly dissipated. Impulsive decisions and momentary pleasures had depleted my bank account, leaving me with nothing substantial to show for it.

A profound realization took root during the chaos and repercussions stemming from my choices. The meticulously crafted external facades proved futile against the internal demons that tormented me.

In 1983, returning to the embrace of my family in Kodiak brought solace and a fresh perspective. It marked an opportunity to rediscover my purpose and realign my priorities.

At that time, as I set forth into a new chapter of my life, my determination to confront my addiction was unwavering. I was fully aware that this journey would pose challenges, but I was prepared to face them head-on. With the unwavering support of my loved ones, a revitalized sense of purpose, and a commitment to self-improvement, I was confident that I could break free from the cycle of emptiness that ensnared me.

Yet, as I embarked on this journey of self-discovery and healing, I firmly believed that meaning can be uncovered. It was my responsibility to seek it out, confront my addiction, and forge a new path illuminated by purpose, joy, and fulfillment.

"Meaningless! Meaningless!" echoes the Teacher. "Utterly meaningless! Everything is meaningless."

Ecclesiastes 1:2,12–14

In the end all was meaningless. Nothing fascinated me anymore except that I was an addict.

The amazing thing about this journey is that God never stopped pursuing me. He was using my religiosity and sin to set me up for the day that He would introduce Himself to me. But all the while, He watched over me and still does today.

"I will refresh the weary and satisfy the faint."

–Jeremiah 31:25

Bible College 1984

Destructive habits continued to cast a shadow over my life, impairing my capacity to express love and respect to the women around me. At this time, the sin of lust was fully developed. My God-given imagination, given over to my sinful desires, was so vivid that I didn't need external imagery any longer. I could make it happen in my mind, in my day, or my night, whatever I wanted. His struggle was steering me away from the person I aspired to become. At the age of 19, I enrolled at St. Paul Bible College, now known as Crown College, with the intention of dedicating a year to studying about God and distancing myself from romantic entanglements. However, the reality proved more complex than simply flipping a switch.

Surprisingly, the Bible College had a significant ratio of three girls to every guy. Despite my resolve to focus solely on my spiritual journey, the challenge of resisting attention and companionship from girls became palpable, particularly given the perception of my attractiveness at the time. During meals, unintentionally attracting a group of girls around my table became a recurrent occurrence, making it increasingly challenging to adhere to my initial plan of avoiding romantic involvement.

This struggle underscored the deep-seated nature of my addiction to both girls and pornography. It became apparent that these distractions hindered my desire to truly know God, leaving me yearning for an authentic connection with Him. Through these experiences and challenges, I came to the realization that achieving genuine fulfillment and an authentic relationship with God required me to confront and overcome my addictive behaviors. However, I have since understood that this belief was misguided, as my own efforts cannot transform my fallen nature. Victory over these challenges can only be found through the grace of God and a genuine relationship with Jesus as my Lord and Savior.

My resolve to avoid romantic entanglements endured for a mere two weeks until I encountered Theresa Kauffman. Our paths crossed during one of my vocal practices, facilitated by one of her close friends with whom I was singing. From the outset of our conversation, it felt like we could discuss anything and everything except for my concealed dark secret.

As I delved deeper into the study of God's Word, I stumbled upon a passage that underscored the significance of marriage to avoid succumbing to burning passion. Within three months, right before the Christmas break, I mustered the courage to propose to Theresa. To my astonishment, she said yes! I couldn't fathom what she saw in me, but she perceived something valuable. However, amid the joy, I grappled with a recurring question. If my mother, father, brother, or sister were to pass away, would I shed a tear? Once again, I found myself inquiring of God, "What is wrong with me?" Little did I know that God had a meticulously crafted plan, unfolding toward a profound revelation.

Chapter 6: Theresa

Theresa entered my life during a private singing rehearsal, and our connection was immediate. Our conversations flowed effortlessly, deepening with time. Following that initial meeting, we found ourselves sharing dreams and fears under the expansive blue sky, laughter filling the air and mingling with the sounds of nature. It was as though the world around us faded, leaving only the two of us in our little cocoon.

As the sun dipped below the horizon, casting a warm glow, Theresa and I reclined on the grass, gazing up at the emerging stars. The tranquil beauty of the evening enveloped us, with the gentle rustle of leaves and distant sounds of nature providing a serene backdrop to our growing connection. Beneath the vast Minnesota sky, the stars danced and sparkled, creating a magical spectacle. Witnessing Theresa's first shooting star became a cherished memory, and each evening brought more opportunities to make wishes and revel in the enchantment of the night sky. With a blanket beneath us and our fingers entwined, time seemed to stand still as we eagerly awaited the streaks of light racing across the starry expanse. The peaceful evenings echoed with our conversations and occasional giggles.

In those moments, we discovered the truth about shooting stars: they are always there, a testament to the wonders of our creator. Minnesota became the backdrop, and I knew she was the one.

Reflecting on my initial attraction to Theresa, I could not deny its shallowness. However, something about her drew me in, and I felt a sense of embarrassment. Theresa's intelligence was undeniable, her with a constant source of amusement and intrigue. Her passion and knowledge spanned a myriad of topics, displaying her understanding of spirituality and her caring nature. It became clear that she might be the one to guide me in the right direction.

She was also a Scrabble enthusiast! Despite my limited spelling abilities compared to her vast vocabulary, winning or losing did not matter to me; being with her brought joy. It served as a delightful distraction from the reality of who I truly was inside. However, as time passed, a growing sense of guilt crept in regarding the superficial nature of my attraction to Theresa. My pornography addiction had influenced my perception of relationships, shaping how I believed a woman should be treated.

This internal conflict intensified as I grappled with the war between striving to do right and succumbing to the pull of sin. Reflecting on my feelings, I recognized the need to be truthful with Theresa. Yet, I found myself unable to confide in her for some inexplicable reason. I questioned whether our connection went beyond surface-level attraction or if I was drawn to the idea of what she represented and her relationship with Jesus.

Theresa played a significant role in my journey of God-discovery and having a relationship with Jesus. Relying on her became a natural inclination. I felt the necessity to delve into her values, dreams, and the intricacies of her character. She was the one who could lead me to God, I thought. Despite spending ample time together and enjoying our conversations, I came across a manipulative nature within me aimed at an ulterior mission. The struggle against hormones and entangled sin persisted. While I liked Theresa, the attraction was not fully genuine, and my desire for her was driven by a preconceived mold of the ideal woman I had constructed.

The institution of marriage is firmly grounded in the Bible and is regarded as a sacred covenant. God orchestrated the concept of marriage, and it is described as a divine covenant between a man and a woman. The foundational account of this institution is found in the book of Genesis, where God brought Adam and Eve together.

"A man shall leave his father and mother and be joined to his wife, and they shall become one flesh."

–Genesis 2: 24

Sexual intimacy is a divine gift designed to become one flesh (a baby) and to strengthen the bond between a man and a woman after marriage. It serves as an expression of love, unity, and the deepest form of communication within the confines of marriage. The values of sexual purity and faithfulness within the marriage covenant are held in high regard. I must confess that I never anticipated the depth of commitment that awaited me.

Three months after our initial meeting, I found myself nurturing a connection with Theresa that exceeded my expectations. Looking back, the Holy Spirit orchestrated her presence in my life, guiding our paths to intersect. Although I had always believed in God, the scriptural truth, "It is better to marry than to burn with passion," resonated with my situation. This realization occurred during one of the intimate moments we shared, and I sensed that this connection was more than mere infatuation. I was determined to approach it with the utmost sincerity.

In my faith, marriage is regarded as a lifelong commitment, with divorce prohibited except in cases of marital unfaithfulness. The core belief is that spouses should navigate challenges together, seeking guidance and support from their community and the Holy Spirit. Uncertain about our future, I made the decision to spend the rest of my life with Theresa.

I understood that love was more than just a word; it encompassed understanding and compassion, binding two individuals together in life. Recognizing that love required numerous thoughtful actions, I knew a proposal should be sweet and unforgettable. Thus, I began crafting various scenarios in my mind.

Theresa had always held a special fondness for KitKat bars, reveling in their layers of chocolaty goodness. It was her guilty pleasure, the one candy bar that could bring a smile to her face even on the gloomiest days. I decided that this particular candy bar held the key to conveying my message to Theresa.

I purchased the KitKat bar and, with gentle hands, unwrapped the chocolate, ensuring that it did not damage the wrapper. The ring, intended to be nestled within the chocolate, was in my possession. With precision, I carefully carved out the bottom of the KitKat bar, creating a hollow space perfectly sized for the plastic case. It was a gesture of great thoughtfulness and adoration, marking the moment when my plan truly began to take shape. This act symbolized the effort I was willing to invest in our relationship. As I wrapped the chocolate bar again, preserving its appearance, I could not help but smile at my creation—a masterpiece of love. I marveled at how well it concealed the secret within.

On the 18th of December 1984, as the frigid wind rustled through the trees from over the lake, Theresa prepared to head home for Christmas in Montana while I planned to visit my grandparents in New Orleans, whom I hadn't seen in thirteen years. With a gaze into Theresa's eyes, I hoped the carefully assembled present would convey my true feelings. In my trembling hands, I held the KitKat bar.

As Theresa opened it, revealing the KitKat bar, she simply said, "Thanks." Putting it away, she had no idea of my plan. Determined, I asked, "Don't you want a piece now?"

She replied, "No, I'll have it later," oblivious to the surprise within. Unwilling to let that happen, I insisted, "No, you want a piece now, not later!" She finally opened it, took a piece, and still remained clueless. It was only when I told her to turn it over that she discovered it was more than a chocolate bar—an engagement ring lay within. Her expression quickly shifted from curiosity to awe, and as she saw the ring, shock left her mouth hanging open for a few moments before the realization sparked in her eyes. Tears welled up as she put on the ring, a promise of my commitment to stay connected, no matter where life's journey took us. I told her that I would always treat her like a queen!

I professed words of love to her, vowing to be with her and care for her for eternity. Leaning over, she kissed me, her lips cold from the winter air. "I will always wear this," she promised me, her voice gentle and full of wonder.

That moment, by the frozen Minnesota lake in our Honda Civic, became forever etched in our memories. A rush of joy, relief, and excitement surged through me as she looked at me and uttered the word I had been so anxious to hear.

SHE SAID YES!

Isn't that a touch of Italian romance? I suppose you had to be there, but I'm glad you weren't.

Chapter 7: Our Marriage

When Theresa and I decided to embark on our marriage journey, we both shared a preference for simplicity. Our wedding preparations were brief, and we chose to celebrate the special day with only our closest and dearest ones.

The much-anticipated moment finally arrived on August 10, 1985, in Kalispell, Montana, where Theresa's family lived. Theresa looked absolutely stunning in her white gown, resembling an angel as she walked down the aisle. A sense of reflection washed over me as we stood together at the altar, exchanging vows.

It became clear to me that I had not been completely honest with myself about my intentions for this marriage. Regrettably, I realized that I was not fully committed to Theresa and that my motivations were not rooted in genuine love. In essence, I was entering into this sacred covenant under false pretenses.

As I uttered the words "I do," an internal conflict raged within me, whispering, "I don't." It dawned on me that my desires were misguided. I was fixated on fulfilling my own needs, using marriage as a means to satisfy my lust rather than understanding the true meaning of love.

I acknowledge now that I was self-centered and shallow, unable to see beyond my own desires. I had unintentionally deceived Theresa, presenting myself as a man of God worthy of her love when, in reality, I was more like a wolf in sheep's clothing, poised to make the most of her innocence.

I recognize the wrongfulness of my actions, the betrayal of trust and commitment. In my weakness, I succumbed to carnal urges, neglecting the potential consequences of my choices. I entered into marriage with Theresa, fully aware that I had yet to grasp the depth of love she truly deserved. In hindsight, I realize my shortcomings as a husband, and I acknowledge the impact this had on her joy.

As the anticipation of our wedding night loomed, I couldn't help but feel a sense of unease. Theresa, a beacon of purity, stood in stark contrast to my imperfect past, which was marked by mistakes and a struggle with certain personal challenges. Our backgrounds and life experiences were distinctly different, and I found it difficult to let go of preconceived notions from my past.

My expectations were not aligned with the reality of our relationship. I sought a certain level of conformity, projecting my desires onto her without considering her own wishes. The stark reality, however, shattered my misguided fantasies.

Theresa, with her gentle nature and innocent charm, found herself in a world vastly different from the one I had known. It became a clash in my heart from the moment we exchanged our vows. My misguided ideals of an ideal woman, influenced by unrealistic images from racy magazines and past experiences, created an unspoken tension. I was fearful at that moment. I did not want to hurt Theresa by backing out, so I continued with the wedding with much turmoil.

As days and months went by, our conflict grew, leading to mounting frustration on both sides. In my attempts to shape Theresa into someone she was not, I tried various approaches; I stole her joy as I manipulated her into the woman on the page.

Reflecting on our situation, I am reminded of a biblical principle:

As mentioned in the Bible, *"Let us love one another, for love comes from God. Everyone who loves has been born of God and knows God."*

8 Just as Jannes and Jambres opposed Moses, so also these men oppose the truth--men of depraved minds, who, as far as the faith is concerned, are rejected.

-2 Timothy 3

I was the latter part of that verse, a man with a deprived mind. I was blinded to the weight of my sin as it pressed heavily upon me. I could not figure out why I could not have a relationship with God and Theresa. I had pushed Theresa to the brink, my relentless demands extinguishing the light in her eyes. She knew she couldn't fulfill my twisted desires, and with the passing of the months, I grew more frustrated. In the depths of my delusion, I even resorted to praying for her demise, a perverse hope that would end my self-inflicted suffering. I had convinced myself that Theresa was the obstacle, the barrier preventing me from reaching my full potential and fulfilling my spiritual calling. This is how perverted I got when sin controlled my life.

I was a narcissist! Shaping every aspect of our life together around my wants and desires. This is the true definition of a narcissist.

My twisted interpretation of scripture fueled my oppressive behavior. I manipulated Theresa with verses like Colossians 3:18

18 Wives, submit to your husbands, as is fitting in the Lord, and the same in Ephesians 5:22, selectively ignoring the broader context of love, respect, and mutual submission. I twisted these verses to justify my control, failing to recognize that true submission stems from within, guided by the Holy Spirit, not imposed by external forces.

For seven lengthy years, I unfortunately imposed the weight of my twisted life on Theresa, blinded by a distorted perspective on marriage and the concept of male supremacy. During that time, I failed to grasp the true essence of marriage—a delicate balance encompassing love and respect. I made her my slave, someone I would use to alleviate my desires. It took years of denial and delusion for me to fully comprehend the gravity of my actions and the profound damage inflicted upon Theresa. Still, at this time, I did not know Jesus. I only knew of him and not the forgiving grace and the power of the Holy Spirit living within. It wasn't until the Holy Spirit opened my eyes later in life that I was truly remorseful.

I acknowledge that I fell short as a husband, a partner, and a fellow human being. My actions betrayed our vows and violated the sacred bond we were meant to share.

Looking ahead, I am committed to carrying the valuable lessons learned from my mistakes and the power of the Holy Spirit in my life, ever mindful of the destructive influence of unchecked ego and the transformative power of genuine repentance. I aspire to be a man of integrity, one who embodies the love, grace, and compassion that Christ exemplified. While Ephesians chapter 5, verse 22 is important, I have come to appreciate the significance of verse 25, urging me to love my wife as Christ loved the church— serving, honoring, and cherishing her rather than demanding submission. It is a commitment to foster an environment where my wife can blossom alongside me.

I have come to recognize that I was the problem in the destructive cycle of constant criticism, hurtful words, and emotional turmoil inflicted on Theresa. This awareness marks the first step toward positive change. Despite my self-awareness, I continued to be ensnared by lust. My earnest desire was to love my wife with the depth and devotion she truly deserved, but I often found myself led astray by my desires, as it says in James 1:14-15.

14 But each person is tempted when they are dragged away by their own evil desire and enticed. 15 Then, after desire has conceived, it gives birth to sin; and sin, when it is full-grown, gives birth to death.

Seeking solace, I turned to prayer, lingering in my self-pity, imploring God to help me uncover the root of my discontent and provide the strength to overcome these persistent temptations.

As I jumped through religious hoops such as prayer, witnessing, and giving my time and money, doing all this was meaningless. I still did not know God. I could not get His attention. I felt trapped in a labyrinth of my own making, unable to escape the clutches of Satan and my evil desires.

In that moment of profound despair, I came to the realization that my struggles were not a result of a lack of God's power but rather my own distorted perception of self. I became increasingly depressed in the seventh year of our marriage. I had wrongly believed that somehow, I could make myself worthy to attain God's acceptance.

The transformation I yearned for was not merely a change in actions or mindset but a reorientation of my heart and a shift in my understanding of God's love and grace. I needed to acknowledge that my worth was not earned but reflected Christ's sacrifice on the cross. It was a concept I had yet to grasp, as my focus at that time was more on head knowledge than becoming a new creation in Christ. I realized that everything that I did to get to God was not working. Hopelessness and anger ascended.

Chapter 8: Standoff with God

Like a scene from a Western movie featuring two gunslingers where one was going to die, and the other lived on, was lined up, there I was before God.

In our eighth year of marriage, I found myself in a storm of depression. And during the last month, I cut myself off from everyone and didn't even talk to Theresa. It was a time of frustration and anger, and in a moment of raw honesty with God, I declared, "If you do not take this lust out of my mind, I am going to leave my wife and children and live out what was in my thought life. At least then, I would not be a hypocrite." I hate hypocrisy, and I hated being one! At that moment, I didn't know if it was my thoughts or the Holy Spirit, but I heard, "But where is there to go?" I knew He was right. I had money. I had a nice car. Before marriage, I had girls. And it was all hollow. No one could live up to my expectations, especially me. Meaningless, all is meaningless.

This prayer, sincere and desperate, scared me. I felt the weight of it, knowing deep down that I was on the edge of doing something drastic. That prayer shook me to the core. I was at my limit, and I could not live my life like this anymore.

After that prayer, I decided to make no more lies and no more striving. He must do it! I was one of those churchgoers who wore a fake smile, hiding the terrible feelings inside. So, I pledged to be truthful.

The decision to be open about my struggles was not just a desperate move but a turning point. It took courage to be honest with myself and those around me.

At that time, I did what some Christians call a lucky dip in the bible. A lucky dip is when you randomly open the Bible, put your finger down, and read whatever verse you land on. In this desperate attempt to hear God, I landed my finger on Romans 15:13, which reads,

"May the God of hope fill you with all joy and peace as you trust in him, so that you may overflow with hope by the power of the Holy Spirit."

This is what I longed for. I needed peace from the turmoil. I needed joy! I needed hope. I needed Him to give me strength to get rid of all this sin.

During this challenging time, some Bible verses brought comfort and guidance. One was Psalm 34:17-18, which said, "The righteous cry out, and the Lord hears them; he delivers them from all their troubles. The Lord is close to the brokenhearted and saves those who are crushed in spirit." This passage reassured me that God heard me even in my darkest moments.

Another verse, James 5:16, urged me to "confess your sins to each other and pray for each other so that you may be healed. The prayer of a righteous person is powerful and effective." It became clear that confessing my sin, not just to God but to others, was a step toward healing.

The journey toward honesty was tough, and Philippians 4:13 became a guiding mantra: "I can do all this through him who gives me strength." It reminded me that my strength came from the Lord.

With each step toward honesty, the burden of hypocrisy began to lift. The weight of maintaining a facade eased, making room for a sense of liberation. It was a journey marked by humility, a willingness to admit my sin, and a deep reliance on God's grace. It was not going to be hidden any longer. I stopped caring what people thought of me. God was the only way!

Confessing my sin became a catalyst for healing, both within myself and in my relationships. The process felt like being refined in the fire, as Zechariah 13:9 describes: "I will refine them like silver and test them like gold." The journey toward authenticity unfolded as a testament to God's redemptive power.

In the echoes of scripture and the transformative power of prayer, this journey became a testament to the enduring truth that God never stopped calling me, even in my moments of deepest deception.

At church, when someone asked how I was doing, I started being honest. "I'm terrible. How are you doing?" I decided to stop hiding and pretending that everything was okay. But when you start telling people at church that you are not okay, they often don't know how to respond.

The turning point came that night after my anger-fueled confrontation with God.

In a moment of clarity, I heard the Holy Spirit say, "But where else is there?"

It hit me hard. I knew He was speaking the truth. Despite being young, having some money, and being a singer, I realized it was all empty. I already had everything that the world had to offer, and I was still hollow. That night, I made a resolution: no more lies. I was going to be honest with Theresa about everything.

However, being truthful meant laying bare the darkest corners of my spirit. That night, I planned to confess to Theresa about my addiction to pornography and the disturbing prayers I made when she and the kids left the house, asking God to end their lives. I was prepared to reveal how wretched I truly was. I knew that any rational person, hearing these things, might think I was irredeemable, that a divorce or separation was the only way out. I was convinced that she would choose that path. Who could love someone like me?

The weight of my confession hung heavy in the air. But I was determined to strip away the layers of deceit and let Theresa see the raw reality of who I was. Even if I lost everything, I had to know God and his power! No one or anything was going to stand in the way!

As I grappled with the decision to be brutally honest, a verse from the Bible lingered in my thoughts: Proverbs 28:13, "Whoever conceals their sins does not prosper, but the one who confesses and renounces them finds mercy." The wisdom in this verse became a guiding light, urging me to step into the uncomfortable territory of confession, trusting in the promise of mercy. I learned the importance of bringing sin to the light. I was going to discover that when I bring sin to the light in my life, it has no hold on me.

The prospect of revealing the depths of my struggles to Theresa was daunting. Yet, I also realized that only by acknowledging the darkness within could I hope for redemption and healing.

The decision to be transparent with Theresa was a leap into the unknown, fueled by a conviction that honesty, even at the risk of losing everything, was the path to genuine transformation. It was God or lose everything.

That night, the truth started, and with a heavy heart, I began to lay bare the demons that haunted my spirit. The confession was raw and unfiltered, and the weight of it hung in the silence that followed.

How she reacted changed me forever. I was cringing in my spirit, waiting for the hammer to come down, knowing that if she knew who I truly was, she would condemn me as I condemned myself.

The revelation of my darkest secrets was met not with judgment but with a depth of compassion and understanding that defied all human logic.

To my astonishment, after about 20 minutes of my confession, she sat up in bed. Her eyes locked onto mine, and with a sincerity that pierced through the darkness, she uttered words that echoed with an unfamiliar kind of love.

"Greg, I love you, and now I know how to help you."

I knew she was hurt, but the love she had for me superseded her broken heart.

Those words, so contrary to my anticipated judgment, left me bewildered. I could not comprehend this kind of love, an unconditional love that defied the logic of my rational expectations. It was the first time that I had seen Jesus in someone else. In that profound moment, for the first time in my life, I saw a glimpse of Jesus through the eyes of my wife, Theresa. It resonated with the scripture that says, "While we were yet sinners, Christ died for us."

Theresa's response echoed the essence of Ephesians 4:32: "Be kind and compassionate to one another, forgiving each other, just as in Christ God forgave you." The love and forgiveness she extended were manifestations of a grace that transcended human understanding.

However, it was not an instantaneous transformation for me. I was not miraculously changed at that very moment. Instead, it marked the beginning of a new journey—a journey where God's love, forgiveness, and grace would gradually weave His transformative threads into the fabric of my being.

With all this, I was still not saved. I saw Jesus in Theresa, but I still did not know Him. What followed next was nothing more than miraculous.

The Song "Erase" was born during a period of deep emotional wounds, reflecting my desperation at the time. Composed amidst tears, I recall sitting on the couch with my guitar, channeling my pain into lyrics. The song emerged from a plea to God to erase these scars, as they were hindering my desire to be with Him above all else. Remarkably, I sensed God responding by singing the same message back to me. It is a profound realization that God longs to be with us even more than we long to be with Him.

Erase

Chapter 9: White Tornado

Just after confessing to Theresa, a friend extended an invitation to attend revival meetings featuring a traveling revivalist, Rodney Howard Brown. These gatherings were no ordinary affairs; they unfolded twice a day, a spiritual rhythm of worship and preaching resonating at ten in the morning and six in the evening. Each service spanned four to five hours.

My desperation was palpable. I found myself in a relentless quest to know God, to break free from the life I had resigned myself to leading. The weight of my impending fate pressed upon me, a fate I knew would plunge me further into the depths of a darker self if God did not come through. The first day I entered that space of spiritual intensity, my prayer was fervent. "I do not care what it takes to get through to me, but you must cleanse my mind. I need to see the power of the cross." It was not a casual plea; it was a desperate cry for transformation because I knew the alternative.

During the services, a singular focus consumed me. As Rodney delivered his message, my internal dialogue with the divine continued: "Lord, I do not care what it takes. You must get through to me." As the Bible says in Acts 1:8.

But you will receive power when the Holy Spirit comes on you, and you will be my witnesses in Jerusalem, and in all Judea and Samaria, and to the ends of the earth."

The hunger for spiritual power, not just to speak the Word but to live it, engulfed my every thought. Not to think sinfully any longer but to be pure in my thoughts and actions. The promise of the Holy Spirit coming upon me echoed in my soul. I recognized the chasm between the life I lived and the life I yearned to embody.

As the culmination of the service approached, Rodney issued an invitation that resonated with the depths of my need. He called forward anyone in need of healing, and at that moment, I recognized the profound healing I sought was not merely temporal but a restoration of my mind, a cleansing of the internal struggles that haunted me.

The call to approach healing became my moment of surrender, a willingness to lay bare my deepest vulnerabilities before the altar of transformation. Stepping into the realm of the revival meeting, I found myself among 20 or 30 others forming a line at the front. Rodney embarked down the line, an embodiment of divine intensity. It seemed as if he was pushing people over, a seeming manifestation of being filled with the Spirit or the fire of divine encounter. It was a phenomenon unfamiliar to me, labeled as being "slain in the Spirit." In this experience, the Holy Spirit descended upon individuals, prompting them to fall under the overwhelming presence of God. In my desperate pursuit of change, I had committed to surrendering to whatever unfolded.

The unfamiliarity of the scene did not deter me; I was willing to do whatever it took to break free from the life I had vowed not to lead. My turn came in this assembly of around five hundred people, joining the collective yearning for spiritual transformation. His hand touched my forehead, and with a gentle yet forceful push, I found myself on the floor. A thought crossed my mind: "Maybe the transformation occurs in the descent." Lying there frustrated, I realized nothing had happened. Anger swelled as I pondered the apparent ineffectuality of the encounter.

Driven by this frustration and anger, I rose abruptly. Rodney, unaware of the turmoil within me, continued to lay hands on people who had come forward. I could not shake the frustration that nothing happened. I didn't want to be touched by man but by God. With determination coursing through my veins, I approached him from behind, tugging hard on his jacket. Startled, he turned to face me, and in that charged moment, I pointed my finger in his face accusingly, declaring, "Nothing happened."

The sudden interruption rippled through the entire service, freezing it at a momentary standstill. The speaker did not realize the depth of my desperation and depression. I stood before him, a man at the crossroads of a life I desperately wanted to escape but lacked the means to do so.

It was an existence I was utterly done with, yet clueless about how to stop myself from its clutches. Regardless, it was my desperate plea for an act of God to intervene and reshape the trajectory of my life. As he turned his attention to me, earnest prayers flowed from his lips. He even tried to get me to laugh. With each uttered word, I felt the breaking of my heart, a poignant realization that the divine touch I longed for had eluded me thus far.

Yet, amidst the unfulfilled expectation, Rodney issued an invitation – return tomorrow morning, for God was doing something. The next morning, I returned to the spiritual crucible.

My wife and I were not only navigating our personal struggles but also serving as youth leaders in the church we attended. Our church also had a school covering students from kindergarten to 12th grade. Remarkably, the school permitted the students to attend these meetings in the morning, creating a unique convergence of spiritual seeking within the younger generation. The service unfolded, and as it reached its culmination, the speaker extended an invitation that hung in the air – anyone desiring to rededicate their life to the Lord should step forward. At that moment, a conflict surfaced within my heart.

Our youth kids were present. Theresa and I were sitting with them. The weight of their potential judgment pressed upon me. What would they think if their youth leader, entrusted with their spiritual guidance, went forward to rededicate his life to the Lord? Yet, a fierce desperation overrode these concerns.

The internal dialogue resonated with urgency: "It doesn't matter. I am desperate. I cannot continue living the life I have been leading." With resolve, I rose from my seat and made my way forward, leaving behind the perceived judgments and focusing on the desperate plea for divine intervention. Desperate people do desperate things!

Led to a back room for prayer, I found myself surrounded by a trio of individuals fervently interceding on my behalf. Amidst this sacred space, a young person behind me attempted to pull me backward, aiming for the sensational experience of being "slain in the spirit."

The touch of man, however well-intentioned, had become wearisome. What I craved was the touch of God, and in that moment, a visceral frustration surged within me. The desire for a divine encounter fueled a fleeting impulse for violence, a visceral urge to turn around and confront the well-meaning but misguided actions. However, I did not act on my feelings. The essence of my desperation lay not in seeking the theatrics of human touch but in yearning for the transformative touch of God Himself.

During the third meeting, a captivating and profoundly symbolic image unfolded within my mind. An almost open vision into which I was transported. I saw a white tornado swirling gracefully within a field of lush, waist-high green grass.

The landscape was breathtaking, surrounded by majestic green trees that added to the overall beauty of the scene—a serene backdrop to the worship and preaching that echoed through the meeting. What struck me most was the purity and beauty of this mental picture.

It stood in stark contrast to the usual mental images that plagued me – images that were putrid, tainted, and far from anything pure. My mind, clouded by the struggles I faced, never entertained pictures that reflected the divine or the beautiful. Satan had me for 30 years at this point.

Yet, in the sanctuary of that meeting, this pristine vision emerged, an oasis of purity during internal turmoil. The significance of this vision became apparent as I reflected on the dichotomy of my thoughts.

In the past, for years, every blink of my eyes or moment of closed eyelids seemed to invite the intrusion of menacing, demoniacal faces. It was a haunting experience that pushed me to adapt to my prayers and even my sleep patterns. Even at this time, at age 30, I was afraid of the dark and still had knight terrors.

I found solace in praying with my eyes open and sleeping with the same vigilance, avoiding the unwelcome invasion of those disturbing images. However, this vision of the white tornado and the verdant field represented a departure from the darkness that overshadowed my thoughts.

It was a glimpse into the purity that emanates from God, a reminder that amidst the chaos of my internal struggles, God could paint a canvas of tranquility and beauty.

This mental image, unlike the sinister faces that haunted me, was a testament to the transformative power of His intervention and the love He has for us all. Here is a song that reflected that moment in time.

Whose Side Are You On

Upon returning for the fourth time, the divine narrative within my mind continued to unfold, adding layers to the vivid imagery that had captivated my thoughts. The familiar scene persisted – the field of lush, waist-high green grass, the white tornado, and the protective embrace of surrounding trees. Yet, with each subsequent visit, God introduced new elements to the mental canvas.

On this occasion, a striking addition emerged – a generous infusion of fire about a quarter of the way from the bottom of the tornado. Focusing on this visual symphony, I found myself in a familiar posture, seeking understanding from Him. "What are you trying to convey, God? What does this mean, God?"

Despite my persistent inquiries, answers remained elusive.

Undeterred, I returned for the fifth time, anticipating further revelation. This time, the entire tornado was ablaze, a mesmerizing dance of twisting fire within the serene field. Engaging in worship like never before, my focus centered on the fiery spectacle, unaware of the profound shift about to occur. Everyone there faded, and it was me and the vision the Lord had placed in my mind.

As the scene unfolded, the tornado suddenly flattened out within the field with violence. The ground shook, exposing rubbish that was hidden in the tall grass. In the turbulence, previously concealed rubbish scattered into the air, exposed by the tumultuous dance of fire. Then, in a moment of abruptness, the tornado retracted and vanished, taking all the rubbish with it.

The suddenness of the event caught me off guard. My eyes closed in intense focus and were startled open. In that instant, a gasp escaped me as I beheld a remarkable sight—scales fell from my eyes and shattered upon the ground.

It was an amazing moment, laden with life-filling significance. As the echoes of the visual revelation lingered, the audible voice of Jesus resonated in my right ear. It was a profound moment, marking the first time I truly heard my God speak. The words spoken penetrated my soul, a message transcending the visual metaphor. *"It was nothing that you could have ever done, but everything I did on the cross; you are now pure."* The weight of those words settled in my heart, a revelation of grace and redemption that transcended human comprehension.

And it was true. I did not do anything to clean myself. I did not jump through any religious hoops to get this. It was not due to any effort from me but a gift.

In that sacred moment, the evolving imagery revealed a spiritual metamorphosis, a purification beyond my own efforts—a divine declaration that purity would become my new reality through the sacrifice on the cross.

What I longed for my whole life was what I had in that moment. I was a New Creation by the grace of God! And this verse came alive. 2 Corinthians 5:17

Therefore, if anyone is in Christ, the new creation has come: The old has gone, the new is here!

For the first time in my life, I had a pure thought, and this new life came alive, and the old was gone forever.

In a moment of surrender, as I embraced God's unconditional love and acceptance, I finally found the freedom I had been desperately seeking. The chains of lust that had bound me for so long lost its grip, replaced by a newfound sense of peace and liberation.

John 15:3-5, where Jesus declares, *"You are already clean because of the word that I have spoken to you... Remain in me, and I will remain in you. As the branch cannot bear fruit of itself, except it abide in the vine, neither can you, except you abide in me."*

By the power of the Holy Spirit, I had a sweet victory over everything that haunted me in an instant. Here is the song that I wrote for this moment. Scan this QR code to listen to it on YouTube. Leave a comment on what you think of the song.

Sweet Victory

Chapter 10: And He Walks with Me, He Talks with Me, and He Tells Me I am His Own

A profound transformation took place as the veil was lifted from my eyes, revealing a new reality. The true reality! The experience bestowed upon me an extraordinary sense of grace and mercy, illuminating my understanding. Empowered by the Holy Spirit, my purified mind enabled me to resist the allure of sin, surrendering my life to Jesus as my Lord.

In relinquishing ownership of myself, a remarkable clarity emerged, dispelling the clutter that once clouded my existence. Instantaneously, a deep love for my wife and children welled up within me, marking a profound shift.

As the metaphorical scales fell away, it was as if an old Rolodex of my life turned, exposing addresses and phone numbers. The scriptures, once merely read and memorized, burst forth with life, akin to the swift rotation of that Rolodex. In an awe-inspiring moment, the desires of a lifetime were fulfilled. I had encountered God, who became my Lord, Savior, King, and confidant. I was saved, and the essence of my existence transformed in an instant. The Word of God was alive! His presence was in me and with me. I could hear His voice with clarity! And His power worked through me!

Right after the event of scales falling off, God, in His divine guidance, gently led me through a series of visions and intimate conversations, unraveling the threads that held the key to healing my strained marriage. With a mind liberated from the shackles of pride and lust, I found myself acutely attuned to the unmistakable voice of the Lord.

In these visions, the Holy Spirit unveiled the painful truth about how I had unwittingly stripped my wife of joy from the very beginning of our relationship. She had endured the weight of an untrustworthy and oppressive husband until this transformative moment.

The initial conversation unfolded with the Holy Spirit urging me to remove my wedding ring— a symbol laden with significance. As I delicately slid the ring off my finger, trepidation and anticipation enveloped me. The exchange resonated with a divine cadence:

"Take off your wedding ring."

A heaviness filled the air as I gingerly complied with trembling fingers.

"Ok."

"Look at it."

"Ok, Lord."

As I gazed upon the ring, a surge of emotion coursed through me—a visual representation of a commitment that had never been luster.

"What does this ring represent?"

A poignant pause lingered, and in that silence, a floodgate of memories and emotions inundated my mind, each moment of our journey together flashing before my eyes.

"It represents the vow I took when I got married."

Although I was stern in my answer, the next question that awaited me was a blow to the core of my heart. The Lord asked me in a commanding yet gentle voice, "What was the vow you made before Me, your wife, and everyone who attended the wedding ceremony?"

The penetrating inquiry cut through me, unraveling layers of complacency that had obscured the essence of my commitment. A carousel of emotions spun within me, memories both tender and painful resurfacing.

I choked on my answer as I remembered the day when we made the vow in front of the Lord. "The vow was to Love, Honor, and Cherish Theresa."

The ring had always felt heavy and hindered me, but the Holy Spirit urged me to view it differently. The Holy Spirit consoled me and gave me hope: "OK, good!

Now, start doing that. You have not loved, honored, and cherished her."

The revelation struck like a thunderbolt, a weighty realization prompting a swell of remorse and a newfound determination.

Although I understood what the Holy Spirit wanted to tell me, I was still uncertain as to how to achieve such a feat. In confusion, I asked Him, "But how do I do that, Lord?"

And the Holy Spirit assured me, "I will show you."

With those words, a profound sense of hope blossomed, and I surrendered to the guidance that promised to reshape my actions and intentions, paving the way for the restoration of a love that had been obscured for far too long.

Continuing the divine encounter, God painted a vivid image in the canvas of my mind—a sizable diamond tarnished and marred with muddy smudges and fingerprints, sitting snugly in the palm of my hand. Devoid of the brilliance and luster one would expect, it failed to radiate the inherent beauty of a diamond.

Inquisitively, I asked, "What is it?"

"It is your wife, and this is what you and others in this world have done to her."

A profound weight settled within me as I absorbed the gravity of the revelation. Eager for guidance, I implored, "Ok, go on."

"Every day, pick this diamond up and breathe on it, wipe it, and clean it."

Perplexed by the method, I questioned again, "How do I do that?"

He declared, "Stare at her."

Perplexity turned to contemplation as I sought clarification, "Just stare at her?"

He reassured me of His support and guidance, "Yes, just stare at her, and I will put the right words in your mouth to say."

It was like a sacred assignment had been given to me—daily acts of intentional observation and cleansing, a symbolic act to restore the brilliance to the metaphorical diamond that was my wife. It became a journey of rediscovery, a commitment to behold her essence with unwavering attention, allowing the divine wisdom to guide my words and actions. Thus, a transformative process began, where the act of staring became a conduit for healing and restoration within the sacred covenant of our marriage.

Embracing the divine directive, I diligently conducted this simple task. Working from home afforded me many opportunities to gaze upon Theresa, and so I started seeking to wipe away the smudges from the metaphorical diamond.

Caught in the act, Theresa would curiously question, "What?"

I would respond simply by saying, "I love you." My response was met with a skeptical hand gesture, a lingering residue of the doubts I had sown. Though she remained unaware of the profound encounters with the divine, she sensed a transformation within me.

Yet, there lingered a need to erase the seeds of mistrust I had sown. I embarked on the journey of rebuilding trust in her heart. Fifteen to twenty minutes later, she would catch me again, prompting her to inquire once more.

"What?" she would ask.

"You are pretty," I would affirm, yet her disbelief persisted. These brief interactions may have seemed trivial, but the Holy Spirit insisted on their continuation.

Repetition became the rhythm of our days—short, sincere affirmations aimed at chipping away at the skepticism rooted in the past. Despite her initial reluctance to believe, the Holy Spirit's guidance served as my unwavering compass.

This cycle of staring and affirming unfolded many times a day, a testament to the persistent commitment to restore and rebuild. Each moment, significant, became a thread in the fabric of trust being woven within the sacred space of our relationship.

A month into doing this strategy, I remember her catching me staring at her, and she said, "What?"

In the dynamics of our evolving connection, the moments of affirmation became the catalyst for a profound transformation. Saying the words "You are beautiful!" carried a resonance that broke through Theresa's usual skepticism, revealing a sparkle in her eyes and a subtle smile—no longer bearing the weight of disbelief.

As the days passed, she began to come alive, and a newfound joy emanated from within her. The commitment to staring and cleansing persisted, and I witnessed her transformation happening right before my eyes.

One month turned into two and then three. In the third month, a divine surprise awaited me. Engaged in the familiar act of staring, Theresa, with a tender voice and an expectant gaze, prompted me to acknowledge her. Tears welled in my eyes as I struggled to find the right words, finally managing to say, "BEAUTIFUL, YOU ARE BEAUTIFUL."

In that moment, I realized that as I sought to erase the seeds of doubt in her, God was simultaneously transforming my own heart. What I had not seen before my conversion experience, He revealed to me now—there's beauty that transcended the physical.

The strategy persisted, and the divine intervention continued to shape our connection. It was not just Theresa's transformation; God's subtle hand was refining my own perceptions. Reflecting on this, I marveled at the sneakiness of His ways.

Even to this day, the strategy of staring and affirming endures—a constant reminder of the beauty that persists within my wife. Gratitude fills my heart as I recognize that I am the most fortunate man on the planet.

Additionally, the Holy Spirit provided another strategy: I was prohibited from wearing sunglasses that obscured my eyes. In the past, I had used mirrored sunglasses to hide my eyes and indulge in lustful gazes. This revelation urged accountability, a stark reminder for men to be vigilant and responsible for the gaze they cast upon others, preserving the sanctity of their relationships.

In the Holy process of God's guidance, another remarkable strategy unfolded, a testament to His limitless creativity. The Holy Spirit gifted me with a unique ability—a divinely imaginative perspective. Blessed with what I affectionately deemed a "crazy God imagination," I found that a divine intent transformed every pretty face I encountered in public.

In a marvel of intervention, God seamlessly overlaid Theresa's image onto theirs, a consequence of the profound staring that had imprinted her features on my mind.

It was a breathtaking revelation—God, unrestrained by limitations, orchestrating strategies that harmonized to bring about transformative change. This extraordinary gift extended beyond my relationship with Theresa; it became a lens through which I learned to honor other women as my sisters.

The guidance found in Matthew 6:22-23 echoed with profound relevance:

"Your eye is the lamp of the body. If your eyes are healthy, your whole body will be full of light. But if your eyes are unhealthy, your whole body will be full of darkness."

The Bible, a reservoir of life's wisdom, illuminated the path forward.

Yet, even amid this discovery, a divine command was issued: "Do not quote scripture to your wife because you have abused my words to manipulate her. Even though I made my word come alive in you, she still does not trust it."

It was a sobering reminder that the transformative power of scripture, while alive within me, the Word of God, through me, needed time to resonate in Theresa's heart. The delicate balance between divine guidance and human understanding unfolded, each revelation weaving into the broader narrative of our journey toward healing and restoration.

During that guidance period, another command from the Lord echoed with purpose: "Do not approach her sexually. Let her come to you." This instruction posed a significant challenge, especially for someone with a history of addiction like me. Despite the inner struggle, the Holy Spirit bestowed upon me the strength to resist my desires, a testimony of His empowering grace that I gratefully acknowledged. This task needed much patience and perseverance, as well as refraining from initiating intimacy and allowing Theresa the space to take the lead. It was a challenging year, marked by periods of waiting, sometimes spanning a month or more before intimacy ensued. Yet, the obedience to this divine command bore fruit beyond measure.

When Theresa did come alive, the marriage bed became a sacred place, infused with a holiness and purity that transcended the earthly realm. It was an experience akin to heaven—though even that fell short of describing the profound depth of connection and intimacy. This divine directive taught a profound lesson: the act of receiving is intricately tied to the ability to give freely. The reminder to refrain from taking allowed for a transformation in the dynamics of our relationship. The principle held true: it is better to give than to receive. When one gives from a heart liberated from manipulation, there are no bounds. Such a heart can offer 100%, not merely from the remnants left behind. This revelation became a cornerstone, emphasizing the significance of a selfless and liberated approach to love and intimacy within the sacred bond of marriage.

Another amazing incident happened during that time when Theresa extended an invitation to go swimming—an activity I had typically avoided due to the potential triggers it held for me. It was about a year into this new life of ours. Reluctant yet committed to serving her, I agreed, trusting her promise to protect me from the distractions that had once troubled me.

Arriving at the club, we were pleasantly surprised to find it deserted. Theresa and I immersed ourselves in the moment, enjoying each other's company. However, we got separated, with her engaging in exercise while I lingered close to the nearby dressing rooms.

Unbeknownst to me, Theresa spotted the potential source of distraction first. When I turned around and encountered the other girl, I found myself ensconced in Theresa's arms. She gently grabbed my head, tilted it down, locked eyes with me, and declared, "I have you!" In that moment, she began to flirt with me playfully, and my heart melted. The love that had blossomed between us was divine, a gift from heaven.

This experience illuminated the truth found in the Genesis verse where God declared, "I will make a help mate for him." The scripture came alive, and I began to experience the living word tangibly. The connection between us transcended earthly understanding, rooted in a profound understanding and commitment nurtured by the divine intervention that had reshaped both our hearts and our marriage.

Here is a song that I wrote called 'Profound.' It is truly profound how putting your faith in Jesus Christ gives you a brand-new life, a brand-new heart, and a brand-new reason to live! Take your phone and scan the QR code to listen to Profound on YouTube.

Profound

Chapter 11: Children's Love and Laughter

In the life before BC (Before Christ), my indifference toward children was palpable—an unsettling sentiment in a world that often celebrates the joy they bring. Theresa, however, held a deep love for them, and for her sake, Stephen and Sharaya were born. However, the scales falling from my eyes brought about an extraordinary transformation, awakening a profound and unexpected love for my children.

Guided by the Holy Spirit, I found a newfound expression of love for my family. Returning home from work or trips, my face would light up with genuine excitement, a testament to the joy that now permeated my life. This joy was not confined to the walls of my home; it extended to everyone I encountered, radiating warmth and genuine care.

A life once overshadowed by depression and hopelessness had morphed into one brimming with joy and the transformative power of God's Word. The haunting images of the past were supplanted by visions of heaven and the Kingdom of God, with my dreams now dominated by His Kingdom.

In this alteration, I realized that I had discovered true reality. The Holy Spirit's voice became audible, and I, by His grace, could comprehend it.

Conversations with the divine transpired a captivating and ongoing dialogue. The presence of the Holy Spirit surrounded me and permeated within, creating an immersive experience without end. This newfound connection with the divine shaped not only my perception of reality but also the very essence of my existence, turning ordinary moments into extraordinary encounters with my Lord, my wife and my children.

As the sands of time continued to flow, Theresa and I discovered a profound love for our adopted children, Douglas and McKayla. In the depths of our hearts, they were not just adoptees; they were our own, and our love for them knew no boundaries.

Coming home became a jubilant occasion, especially for these younger members of our family. The moment I stepped through the door, they would rush into my arms, laughter and joy filling the air. We would gather, with each child finding a place on a knee, creating a scene of familial unity and love.

Inspired by the newfound depths of our affection, Theresa and I felt called to open our hearts even wider, embracing foster care. This decision was born out of a desire to extend the transformative love we had experienced to those who had never felt such warmth before. Little did we anticipate the challenges and rewards this choice would bring.

The decision to foster care, while noble, brought with it its own set of difficulties. However, with the Holy Spirit residing within us, we navigated through the challenges. The divine presence guided us, providing strength and wisdom as we sought to share love and stability with those who needed it most. Each hurdle became an opportunity for growth and learning, further solidifying our commitment to creating a home filled with love, grace, and the enduring presence of the Holy Spirit.

Through the journey of foster care, two extraordinary children, Suzy-Q and Douglas, entered our lives, adding immeasurable joy and depth to our family. Suzy-Q, a bright four-year-old, was part of a group of seven siblings, the oldest merely seven years old and shouldering the responsibility of caring for the others. Their living conditions were dire, lacking proper hygiene and adequate food. When Suzy-Q came into our care, she was initially reserved, observing from a distance as Stephen and Sharaya would light up in my presence.

Gradually, a transformation happened. Suzy-Q, once a hesitant observer, began competing for my lap and, in doing so, discovered the magic of her own laughter. Her infectious joy became a catalyst, spreading through our home and bringing laughter to every corner. The once-muted atmosphere changed into one filled with the sounds of genuine happiness.

Douglas, the second foster child to join our family, arrived at just six months old, having endured severe abuse and initially displaying no emotions. His journey toward healing and joy was profound. As he discovered his laughter, it became a wellspring of immense joy not only for him but for our entire family. Every Sunday at church, he became a beacon of happiness, circulating from hand to hand as everyone wanted to hold him close.

Our love for these foster children ran so deep that we chose to adopt Douglas, and he has grown into an incredible young man. His story stands as a powerful testimony to the transformative and healing power of love and laughter. Through fostering and adopting, our family expanded not just in numbers but in the richness of shared experiences, becoming a living testament to the boundless capacity of the human heart to heal and embrace others with love.

Among the myriad of transformative stories that could fill an entire book, let's delve into the strategies that have become integral to my journey—a unique set bestowed upon me by the Holy Spirit. While different strategies may guide your path, these insights might serve as a valuable starting point.

These strategies, while deeply personal, underscore the diverse and tailored approaches the Holy Spirit may provide to individuals. They are a testament to the multifaceted nature of transformation and the unique ways in which divine guidance can shape and enrich our lives.

This is a song that I wrote after one and a half years of my transformation. Let me know what you think.

I Love This Life

Chapter 12: Strategies for Breaking Addiction

In every strategy, the guiding principle remains rooted in 2 Corinthians 10:4-5. As it proclaims,

"The weapons we fight with are not the weapons of the world. On the contrary, they have the divine power to demolish strongholds. We demolish arguments and every pretension that sets itself up against the knowledge of God, and we take captive every thought to make it obedient to Christ."

This scripture underscores the divine power inherent in the strategies provided by the Holy Spirit. These strategies, crafted to break the chains of addiction, particularly in my case, pornography, serve as potent examples of the Holy Spirit's ability to lead individuals into freedom. Addiction, a pervasive challenge, comes in various forms, yet the promise remains—those who earnestly seek the Holy Spirit's guidance can find liberation. As scripture declares, *"It was for freedom that Christ has set us free." Galatians 5:1.*

Addictions are, at their core, objects of worship. We, as humans, were created to worship, and the call is to redirect that worship toward its rightful place—God. The strategies provided are not just tools for breaking free from addiction; they are pathways to reorienting our worship, placing it in alignment with the divine purpose for which we were created.

Strategy #1: Desperation to Know God

The foundational strategy revolves around cultivating a desperate desire to know God. Recognizing Him as the Alpha and Omega, the beginning and the end, underscores the transformative potential inherent in surrendering one's life to Him. This strategy, previously explored in earlier chapters, emphasizes the profound shift that occurs when individuals wholeheartedly give themselves to God, and trust God with their whole life.

The journey of desperation to know God is a journey of discovery—a discovery of an incredible new life that unfolds when God becomes the center. The Alfa and Omega, symbolic of God's all-encompassing presence, signify that the transformative process begins and ends with Him. This strategy serves as the cornerstone, urging individuals to relinquish control and embrace the divine, setting the stage for a life marked by renewed purpose and profound connection.

Strategy #2: Embrace Freedom from Condemnation

Drawing inspiration from Romans 8:1, this strategy revolves around embracing the liberating truth that there is no condemnation for those in Christ Jesus. Understanding that through Christ, the law of the Spirit has set us free from the law of sin and death is pivotal for breaking the chains of condemnation.

The challenge lies in comprehending this concept, as societal norms and personal beliefs often dictate a need to pay for wrongdoing. However, the revelation is uplifting, as Jesus has already paid the full price on the cross. When we stumble or err, the path to redemption involves turning away from our sins through repentance and accepting His forgiveness. This can be arduous, given our inclination to self-condemn and engage in self-flagellation, perpetuating a pattern from countless past instances.

The question arises: If Jesus paid the entire price on the cross, do we still bear any burden? Firmly anchored in the belief that "all" means all, scripture suggests that when we sin and repent, we can walk as though we have never sinned. While this notion may challenge the human spirit, putting it into practice through faith unveils a gradual decrease in the frequency of our falls. It becomes a transformative process, a journey of living out our faith.

Distinguishing between godly sorrow and condemnation is crucial. Godly sorrow leads to repentance and positive change, while condemnation only serves to keep us entangled in guilt and shame. Embracing freedom from condemnation is not just a theological concept; it is a practical strategy that, when lived out in faith, paves the way for a life marked by repentance, forgiveness, and the transformative power of God's grace.

Initially, the notion felt peculiar, but over time, I witnessed Jesus gaining victory over my life. A persistent addiction to labeling myself as stupid or incapable, a mindset ingrained before my encounter with Christ, began to crumble.

Philippians 4:8 served as a guiding light, urging a shift in focus toward things that are true, noble, right, pure, lovely, admirable, excellent, and praiseworthy.

Confronting thoughts of inadequacy, whether internal or spoken aloud, became an opportunity to counteract them with the truths found in God's Word. Affirmations like "I am lovely, intentionally created before the foundations of the earth, intricately formed in my mother's womb—therefore, no one is a mistake" became powerful weapons against the lies that once held sway.

Gradually, the process revealed a reflective transformation—I was being rebuilt on a foundation of truth, dismantling the falsehoods that others had spoken over me and that I had once spoken over myself. This recalibration of thought proved pivotal, especially in the context of addiction. Replacing self-condemning thoughts with the liberating truth of God's Word became a cornerstone of the journey toward freedom. As scripture assures, "The truth will set you free."

However, a crucial caution arises—the understanding that embracing freedom from condemnation does not license one to sin to seek repentance freely. Such a mindset hints at a lack of sincerity in understanding Jesus.

Those aspiring to emulate their heavenly Father should embrace the purity bestowed by Jesus, with actions driven by a sincere desire to please those they love rather than viewing repentance as a mere religious practice. A genuine relationship and a heart earnestly seeking to align with divine principles should be the driving force behind one's actions.

Strategy #3: Bring Sin into the Light

A crucial strategy involves bringing sin into the light, for in doing so, Satan loses his grip. The act of hiding or concealing is attributed to the devil, and this strategy calls for courage to expose one's deepest and darkest secrets. Desperation becomes the driving force to find someone trustworthy to confide in, recognizing that concealing sins only empowers the enemy. As Numbers 32:23 warns, *"Your sin will find you out,"* emphasizing the need to confront it head-on.

However, discretion is key. Not everyone needs to know; instead, carefully choose one or two trusted friends or a spouse. This selective sharing is not about airing one's dirty laundry to all but prayerfully considering who would be the right individuals to bring into the circle of healing. The principle of "dumping up, not down" holds true—turn to pastors or mature Christians for support. If you are a man, confide in a man; if you're a woman, confide in a woman. Wisdom guides this process, recognizing the importance of walking in discernment and seeking the right individuals to provide genuine support and understanding.

Strategy #4: Confronting the Lust of the Eyes

Addressing the lust of the eyes, a seemingly mundane accessory became a symbol of significant transformation—sunglasses. In the past, I wore mirrored sunglasses as a shield, allowing me to gaze and lust after other women without revealing my intentions. However, the Holy Spirit called for a radical shift—abandoning this protective barrier.

The symbolism embedded in relinquishing mirrored sunglasses was very insightful. It marked a conscious decision to embrace vulnerability and accountability. No longer could I hide behind the tinted shield that concealed my intentions. It became a tangible act of submission to God's guidance, an acknowledgment of the necessity to expose my eyes to His transformative light.

The absence of sunglasses became a daily reminder of this commitment. With unobstructed eyes, I walked around a world that no longer afforded the shadows of secrecy. The vulnerability was discomforting initially, laying bare the areas where darkness had previously thrived. Yet, I found the space for growth and redemption in this discomfort.

This strategy underscores the importance of bringing sin to the light and staying out of the shadows. By confronting the lust of the eyes and abandoning protective measures, a pathway to genuine transformation and accountability emerges.

As I faced the world with unfiltered eyes, the reality of my past actions and the consequences of my choices became starkly apparent. The once-hidden corners of my heart were now exposed to the cleansing light of God's grace. It became a journey of self-discovery and repentance, a conscious effort to align my gaze with the principles of love and fidelity.

The Holy Spirit's guidance in discarding sunglasses became more than a simple act – it was a shedding of old, distorted lenses through which I had viewed the world. The mirrored shields, once tools for secrecy and indulgence, were replaced by newfound transparency. This shift was a declaration of accountability, a commitment to guard my eyes against the temptations that had trapped me.

For every man entangled in the web of mirrored sunglasses, the Holy Spirit's counsel echoes – stop. The call is not merely to discard a physical accessory but to dismantle the metaphorical barriers obstructing the path to purity. It is an invitation to be accountable for your eyes, recognizing that the potential for renewal and restoration lies in the vulnerability of an exposed gaze. This serves as a powerful reminder that the revolution journey involves tangible actions and a deliberate shift in perspective, aligning one's vision with the purity and clarity found in God's transformative light.

Strategy #5: Embrace Accountability within a Faithful Community

Building on the importance of accountability, the next strategy emphasizes the significance of finding a God-fearing, Bible-teaching church community. Beyond being accountable to friends and a spouse, being part of a faith community offers additional layers of support and guidance. In the diverse landscape of churches, many congregations will embrace individuals seeking spiritual growth.

Commitment to a church community becomes pivotal, offering a consistent and nurturing environment for spiritual development. It is a place where one can find both support and challenge, essential components for personal and communal growth. By actively engaging in such a community, individuals can draw strength from shared faith, collective wisdom, and the teachings that align with biblical principles.

Complementing the need for commitment is our next strategy on the list.

Strategy #6: Reject Self-Pity

The sixth strategy is a resolute call to reject self-pity. It highlights the insidious nature of self-pity, which can masquerade as humility but is, in fact, false. This concept resonates closely with Strategy #4, focusing on how one perceives oneself, akin to the Eeyore syndrome—life is unfair, woe-is-me, people owe me. These attitudes are tactics the devil employs to keep individuals trapped in a mindset of victimhood.

The fundamental message is clear: the world does not owe you anything, and God doesn't owe you anything. Instead, by His grace, He gives—unmerited favor and undeserved life to those who earnestly pursue Him. When ensnared by addiction, the tendency is to blame external factors for one's condition—parents, circumstances, or the actions of others.

The strategy underscores a profound truth: hurt people hurt people. In contrast, God extends grace, and we are called to do the same in return. Forgiveness becomes a transformative act, not just for others but for oneself. By forgiving as Jesus forgave, individuals liberate themselves from the chains of resentment and self-pity. This brings healing and serves as a powerful testament to the transformative power of grace and a commitment to live in the freedom of the new covenant.

Strategy #7: Replace Bad Habits with Good Ones

The seventh strategy promotes the intentional replacement of bad habits with good ones, drawing inspiration from James 1:19-20:

"Know this, my beloved: let every person be quick to hear, slow to speak, slow to anger; for the anger of man does not produce the righteousness of God."

This strategy underscores the importance of cultivating positive habits that align with the virtues highlighted in the scripture—being quick to listen, slow to speak, and slow to anger. Embracing the perspectives of others, rooted in humility, becomes a practice that contributes to spiritual growth.

Constructive criticism, especially from those unafraid to speak the truth, serves as an opportunity for self-reflection. Responding defensively contradicts humility, and instead, individuals are encouraged to embrace the discomfort of self-examination. Avoiding quick comebacks becomes crucial in creating space for the transformative work of the Holy Spirit, allowing His comfort to permeate throughout the process of personal and spiritual growth in Christ.

Strategy #8: Transform Manipulation into Selfless Service

The eighth strategy addresses the insidious nature of manipulation that often accompanies addiction. Recognizing that addiction turns individuals into manipulators, the strategy calls for a conscious effort to relinquish this joy-stealing habit to the Holy Spirit. The transformative shift involves asking the Holy Spirit to open one's eyes whenever manipulating, acknowledging it as a selfish act that needs to be surrendered.

To counter manipulation, the strategy suggests adopting a servant's role. By becoming a servant to those around you, there is no room for manipulation, as true service is selfless. The scriptural foundation for this approach is found in Matthew 20:26-28:

"Instead, anyone aspiring to greatness among you must adopt a servant's role, and those seeking to be first should embrace a mindset of being a slave—just as the Son of Man came not to be served but to serve, offering his life as a ransom for many."

Regular self-assessment is crucial. When engaging in service, it prompts individuals to examine their motives—is it primarily for personal benefit or the genuine well-being of the person being served? This strategy encourages a paradigm shift from manipulation to selfless service, aligning one's actions with the example set by Jesus.

Strategy #9: Be Open to Correction

The ninth strategy emphasizes the importance of being correctable, drawing wisdom from Proverbs 15:31-33:

"Whoever heeds life-giving correction will be at home with the wise. Those who disregard discipline despise themselves, but the one who heeds correction gains understanding. Wisdom's instruction is to fear the LORD, and Humility comes before honor."

In relationships with a spouse or friend who shares a faith-filled life, maintaining an understanding that they genuinely have your best interests at heart is crucial. This mindset facilitates an openness to accept correction or even rebukes from them. True humility, as depicted in this strategy, is not about weakness or permitting mistreatment; rather, it involves approaching all situations with a genuine willingness to learn and grow.

While these nine strategies may seem challenging, earnestly seeking the Lord's presence, drawing strength from the Holy Spirit, and allowing oneself to be corrected lead to empowerment in living them out. Perfection may remain elusive, but a noticeable shedding of sin occurs as one faithfully pursues these principles, marking a transformative journey toward spiritual growth and personal development.

SUMMARY:

In this chapter, I share strategies bestowed upon me by the Holy Spirit to break free from addiction, particularly my struggle with pornography. Grounded in 2 Corinthians 10:4-5, the overarching theme emphasizes the divine power available to demolish strongholds and bring about freedom. The strategies include a desperate pursuit of knowing God, understanding the freedom offered through Christ, and bringing sin into the light through trusted accountability.

Recognizing the significance of repentance and the forgiveness already paid for by Jesus, I discuss the importance of replacing self-condemning thoughts with God's truth. Strategy #3 encourages openness about sin, emphasizing the need for trustworthy confidants. Strategy #4 urges accountability for the lust of the eyes, symbolized by discarding mirrored sunglasses to embrace vulnerability.

Being accountable not only to friends but also to a God-fearing church forms Strategy #5. Strategy #6 warns against self-pity and encourages forgiveness, highlighting the importance of living out the grace we receive. Strategy #7 emphasizes replacing bad habits with good ones, while Strategy #8 focuses on serving others to counteract manipulation.

Strategy #9 underscores the value of being open to correction, recognizing it as a path to wisdom and humility. Collectively, these strategies provide a comprehensive guide for breaking free from addiction, encouraging readers to seek the Lord's presence and find empowerment through the faithful pursuit of these principles and His presence.

Chapter 13: Godly Marriage & Relationships

At the core of each strategy lies the anchoring wisdom of 2 Corinthians 10:4-5:

"The weapons we fight with are not the weapons of the world. On the contrary, they have the divine power to demolish strongholds. We demolish arguments and every pretension that sets itself up against the knowledge of God, and we take captive every thought to make it obedient to Christ."

These verses serve as a compass for revitalizing marriage, unveiling the divine potency behind the strategies bestowed by the Holy Spirit. As I embraced Christianity, the Holy Spirit revealed these strategies to me through visions, images, and verses, offering guiding lights for a transformed life. These are the strategies that the Lord gave me. Yours may be different as you seek His face.

A pivotal moment occurred during a heartfelt conversation with the Holy Spirit, where the significance of my wedding ring took center stage. It became clear that the ring was not just a piece of metal; it symbolized vows to love, honor, and cherish. The Lord's instruction echoed loudly: live by those vows. With a gentle promise of further guidance, I was told to gaze at my wife, initiating a transformational journey.

Following this divine guidance, every uttered "I love you" and "You are beautiful" became not just words but threads weaving a path of renewal. Each sentiment was a brushstroke, painting a portrait of affection and affirmation. In these simple affirmations, I witnessed a tangible shift in my wife. My wife, once questioning my actions, gradually accepted these expressions, and in her eyes, a spark of belief kindled.

Her newfound belief in those words and the sparkle in her eyes painted a beautiful transformation. Little did I realize that, simultaneously, the Holy Spirit was at work in my own heart, unraveling the depth and meaning of the vows I had made. The vows I had made, once recited conventionally, now resonated with newfound depth. This journey of divine strategies was not just about transforming a marriage; it was an excavation of the heart's chambers, uncovering the genuine meaning and commitment embedded in those sacred vows.

In the sequel to these divine revelations, a second vision came to me, painting a vivid image on the canvas of my spiritual journey. The scene unfolded with a large, dull, and dirt-laden diamond, bearing the marks of fingerprints scattered across its once radiant surface. As I gazed upon this symbol, the Holy Spirit's gentle voice resonated, revealing that this diamond embodied Theresa and the collective impact of both my actions and the world's treatment of her.

The analogy struck a chord deep within me, serving as a visual representation of the tarnished beauty that life's challenges had cast upon my wife. The Holy Spirit, the divine artist in this metaphorical masterpiece, urged me to take up the diamond daily. The directive was simple—breathe on it, engage in the deliberate act of cleansing, and board on the transformative process of polishing away the stains that life had engraved onto this precious gem.

The prospect of this task ignited a sense of purpose within me. It wasn't just about cleaning a diamond; it was a tangible expression of commitment to address the hurts I had unintentionally inflicted upon my wife. The daily ritual of picking up the diamond became a ritual of love, a conscious effort to erase the marks of past mistakes and offer a renewed brilliance to the woman I had vowed to love.

In this vision, emotions swirled between the acknowledgment of faults, the eagerness for redemption, and the quiet joy of being entrusted with the responsibility to restore what was once pristine. The Holy Spirit, like a skilled craftsman, guided me through each step of this process, unveiling a path of healing and renewal that echoed beyond the dominion of the metaphor.

This diamond of redemption became more than a visual metaphor; it became a lived reality. Each day, as I engaged in the intentional act of restoration, the once-dull diamond began to reflect a polished radiance. The fingerprints of past shortcomings gradually yielded to the transformative touch of love and dedication. It was a journey of polishing away the stains, a journey of redemption. The symbolism was not lost on me—it was a tangible expression of my commitment to cherish and restore the precious gem that was Theresa, my wife.

After that, a distinctive revelation from the Holy Spirit came to me, guiding me away from the shadows of sunglasses that concealed my eyes. This divine directive held a very deep significance, emphasizing the transformative power of making eye contact—a gesture of openness and honesty with both our loved ones and the world around us.

In the era before my encounter with Christianity, I had a habit of obscuring my eyes with sunglasses. This concealment served as a shield, allowing me to indulge in lustful thoughts while keeping my intentions veiled. It was a deceptive play of desires, a way of satisfying the cravings of my flesh. However, the Holy Spirit, with gentle authority, redirected my gaze toward a different path.

The symbolism within this revelation was poignant. It was not just about forsaking a pair of sunglasses; it was a commitment to unveil my eyes, letting them be a reflection of sincerity and transparency. This shift signified a departure from the shadows of secrecy that once dominated my gaze. It was an acknowledgment of the importance of visibility, not just to others but to God, who sees the depths of our hearts.

The decision to refrain from wearing sunglasses became a daily reminder of this commitment. It was a conscious choice to keep my eyes perpetually visible— a testimony to the transformed intentions within. The journey of discarding the shades mirrored the broader change within my soul, where the once-hidden corners were now bathed in the illuminating light of authenticity.

Embracing this revelation brought forth quite different emotions altogether. There was the discomfort of exposing vulnerabilities, the liberation of breaking free from deceptive habits, and the joy of embracing a newfound clarity. This simple act of avoiding sunglasses became a tangible expression of the desire to live authentically, aligning my vision with the principles of love and fidelity.

In this commitment to transparent vision, I discovered that true freedom lies in the openness of our gaze. It was a lesson in vulnerability, a reminder that honesty not only enriches our relationships but also deepens our connection with the divine. The shadows of secrecy were replaced by the radiance of transparent vision, a testament to the transformative journey orchestrated by the guidance of the Holy Spirit.

The implications of these seemingly simple strategies continued to affect my relationship with my wife, all under the guiding hand of the Holy Spirit. In these divine revelations, I found myself navigating the transformative currents of love, honor, and cherish, discovering their immense power within the sanctity of marriage.

As men, the clarion call resonated through the corridors of our souls—to recognize that a vow is not merely a spoken commitment but a sacred and unbreakable covenant. It stands as a testament before God Himself, carved in the spiritual fabric that binds two lives together. Promises may falter, but a vow remains steadfast, tethered to the divine orchestration of marital unity.

Let us delve into the meanings of Love, Honor, and Cherish, each term carrying its own weight and significance.

Strategy #1: Love

Love, as unveiled in the sacred context of marriage, resonates with depth and transformative power—a force beautifully articulated in 1 Corinthians 13:4-8.

"Love is patient, love is kind. It does not envy, it does not boast, it is not proud. It does not dishonor others; it is not self-seeking; it is not easily angered, and it keeps no record of wrongs. Love does not delight in evil but rejoices with the truth. It always protects, always trusts, always hopes, always perseveres. Love never fails. But where there are prophecies, they will cease; where there are tongues, they will be stilled; where there is knowledge, it will pass away."

These verses portray love as a patient and kind orchestrator, shunning envy, boasting, and pride. It stands as a bulwark against rudeness and self-centeredness, steadfastly resisting the allure of quick anger and the subtle allure of maintaining a tally of wrongs. Love takes no delight in wrongdoing but finds its joy in embracing truth. It possesses an extraordinary capacity to bear, believe, hope, and endure everything. Most importantly, love unfurls its wings in the eternal assurance that it never fails.

To internalize and breathe life into these principles within our daily lives, the practice of memorizing 1 Corinthians 13:4-8 assumes a pivotal role. This act goes beyond mere recitation; it is a deliberate choice to etch the virtues of love onto the canvas of our souls, aligning our intentions with the divine blueprint laid out by the Lord.

Strategically placing this scripture in prominent locations, whether it be on mirrors reflecting our visage each morning, adorning front doors welcoming us home, or present in common sightlines where our gaze naturally falls, serves as a perpetual reminder to uphold the sanctity of love in our interactions.

This is not a mere routine; it is a conscious effort to immerse ourselves in the very essence of love as defined by God. Each day begins with encountering these words, setting the tone for a marriage adorned with the threads of patience, kindness, and enduring love. By embedding these principles into the fabric of our existence, we align ourselves with the divine architecture for marital fulfillment meticulously outlined in the sacred scriptures. In this deliberate choice, we develop the wings of love, allowing it to soar through the corridors of our marriages and resonate with the eternal echoes of God's design.

Strategy#2: Honor

The cornerstone of a flourishing marriage lies in the commitment to honor one's spouse, an indispensable element illuminated in Ephesians 5:25-33.

"Husbands, love your wives, just as Christ loved the church and gave himself up for her to make her holy, cleansing her by the washing with water through the word, and to present her to himself as a radiant church, without stain or wrinkle or any other blemish, but holy and blameless. In this same way, husbands ought to

love their wives as their own bodies. He who loves his wife loves himself. After all, no one ever hated their own body, but they feed and care for their body, just as Christ does the church—for we are members of his body. 'For this reason, a man will leave his father and mother and be united to his wife, and the two will become one flesh.' This is a profound mystery—but I am talking about Christ and the church. However, each one of you also must love his wife as he loves himself, and the wife must respect her husband."

This scriptural guidance implores husbands to mirror Christ's active love for the church, transcending passivity to sacrificial devotion. The vision embedded in this passage is a second revelation from the Holy Spirit, emphasizing the husband's pivotal role in nurturing the spiritual growth of his wife.

The analogy of Christ's transformative love for the church becomes a beacon, guiding husbands to strive toward their wives' holiness.

Cleansing them with the power of God's Word, the objective is to present them as radiant, blameless, and without blemish. This resonates deeply, portraying the spouses as integral members of each other's bodies, highlighting the unity and interdependence within the marital relationship.

Manifesting honor involves a conscious effort to abstain from behaviors that undermine the sanctity of marriage.

Engaging in lustful thoughts about other women, belittling one's wife, incessantly pointing out flaws, and maintaining a record of wrongs all contribute to the erosion of honor within the marriage. Such actions stand in stark contrast to the selfless love exemplified by Christ.

By embracing the understanding that Christ's mission was one of service, husbands are reminded of their divine calling within the marital bond. This realization extends to those in Christ, recognizing that marriage is not a platform for self-indulgence but an opportunity to serve one's spouse.

This aligns with the timeless concept presented in Genesis, where the woman is described as a willing helpmate. The embrace of sacrificial love modeled by Christ contributes to a reciprocal dynamic within the marriage, fostering an atmosphere of mutual service and support.

In this practical application of honor, the marital bond becomes a testament to selfless devotion and shared commitment.

Strategy#3: Cherish

Looking into the principle of cherishing our spouses, as illuminated in Ephesians 5:29, unveils a depth of love that extends beyond mere affection.

"After all, no one ever hated their own body, but they feed and care for their body, just as Christ does the church."

The Greek term for "cherishing," meaning "keeping warm" or "nourishing," places a weighty responsibility on husbands to ensure their wives' holistic well-being. This scriptural guidance becomes the cornerstone for forging resilient marriages capable of weathering any storm.

To authentically cherish one's wife involves a sustained focus on her well-being, encompassing both the physical and emotional realms. A divine revelation emphasized the importance of fixing my thoughts on my wife continually. This intentional practice imprinted her image on my heart, serving as a protective shield in moments when other women crossed my path. The deliberate act of cherishing her as a radiant and beloved woman establishes a safeguard, preserving the sanctity of the relationship even in solitary moments. The result is a love that is not easily shaken but instead deepens over time.

In conclusion, the awareness of strategic attacks launched by Satan against marital bonds is paramount.

The need for godly strategies dispels the deceptive belief that love will sustain itself without intentional effort. Starting with a focused relationship with God and extending to the prioritization of one's wife, family, and others, this intentional approach not only guards against destructive influences but also leads to a fulfilling life marked by overflowing joy.

Undoubtedly, challenges and trials will arise in the pursuit of these strategies. Yet, the resilience cultivated through intentional love and divine guidance empowers couples to withstand the devil's wiles, allowing God to expand their love within the Kingdom continually. The limitless nature of love finds its home in the boundless expanse of God's Kingdom.

Strategy#4: Lay Down Your Life for Your Wife and Others

Contemplating the notion of laying down one's life for a spouse and others may elicit questions about personal happiness and entitlement. However, the stern reality is that life itself is a gift, and the Holy Spirit bestows true comfort and joy, a truth underscored by Jesus in Luke 9:23.

"Then he said to them all: Whoever wants to be my disciple must deny themselves and take up their cross daily and follow me."

Embracing the call to deny oneself and take up the cross daily, as Jesus urged, might seem counterintuitive in a culture that champions self-preservation. Yet, the wisdom in Matthew 10:39 (AMP) illuminates the profound principle that by relinquishing our lives for Christ's sake, we discover a richer, eternal life. This sacrificial approach echoes the very path that Jesus walked.

"Whoever finds his life [in this world] will [eventually] lose it [through death], and whoever loses his life [in this world] for My sake will find it [that is, life with Me for all eternity]."

Choosing not to protect oneself aligns with the essence of faith, where God serves as both protector and provider. The selfless act of serving others and surrendering one's life mirrors the example set by Jesus. In this surrender, God not only lifts our burdens but replaces them with a joyful responsibility.

The paradox of losing our lives results in the discovery of the fruits of the Spirit—love, joy, peace, patience, kindness, goodness, faithfulness, gentleness, and self-control, as beautifully expressed in Galatians 5:22-23.

"But the fruit of the Spirit is love, joy, peace, forbearance, kindness, goodness, faithfulness, gentleness and self-control. Against such things, there is no law."

These virtues emanating from a life laid down signify a life truly fulfilled.

"Come to me, all you who are weary and burdened, and I will give you rest. Take my yoke upon you and learn from me, for I am gentle and humble in heart, and you will find rest for your souls. For my yoke is easy, and my burden is light."

In the verses of Matthew 11:28-30, we encounter a compassionate invitation extended to those burdened and weary. It promises rest for souls seeking solace. As we explore the intricate dynamics of marriage, the act of aligning priorities assumes a position of paramount importance.

"Husbands, love your wives, just as Christ loved the church and gave himself up for her."

According to Ephesians 5:25, your wife is to hold a position just below your relationship with God, forming a lasting and foundational hierarchy.

Let's take a look into the simplicity and profundity of a prioritized life through a straightforward chart:

1. God

2. Wife

3. Children

4. Church

5. Community

The beauty lies in the simplicity of this hierarchy, echoing the principles outlined in Matthew 20:28 and 16:24-25:

"Just as the Son of Man did not come to be served, but to serve, and to give his life as a ransom for many. Then Jesus said to his disciples, whoever wants to be my disciple must deny themselves and take up their cross and follow me. For whoever wants to save their life will lose it, but whoever loses their life for me will find it."

Here, Jesus emphasizes the need to serve and prioritize in a specific order. In this context, the call is not only to prioritize but to do so in a manner that aligns with divine principles.

At times, you might find yourself wondering where you fit into this chart. You are not on the chart because you are a servant to everyone on the list. It is a profound mystery, but you find true joy in serving. This prioritization serves as a reflective journey toward freedom. It's an intentional practice of denying oneself, taking up the cross, and following Jesus—an emulation of His selfless service.

The prioritization aligns with a vision where everyone lives out of these priorities. Imagine a world where individuals embrace the call to serve in the order of God first, wife second, children third, the church fourth, and the community fifth. It becomes a blueprint for a world that mirrors divine priorities—a vision of heaven on earth.

Maintaining this order safeguards against imbalances that can strain marriages and lives. By serving in this divine order, you not only discover a life rich in purpose but also contribute to the creation of a world harmonized with God's design. This simple yet profound structure emerges as a key to marital success and a life filled with meaning and fulfillment.

Strategy#5: Bring to Light

In the journey toward a thriving marriage, the fifth strategy serves as a beacon of transparency—a practice rooted in courage and illuminated by the empowering presence of the Holy Spirit.

"I can do all this through him who gives me strength."

Philippians 4:13 becomes the guiding force, assuring that through Christ, strength emerges for all things, even the courageous act of bringing everything into the light.

In this strategy, the notion of transparency takes a definite form:

1. Share Passwords: An act of vulnerability, sharing passwords dismantles the barriers that secrecy can erect. By entrusting your wife with access to your digital world, you not only foster trust but also eliminate potential hiding places for destructive habits.

2. *Expose Hidden Facets:* Extend access beyond passwords; grant your wife permission to explore any areas where secrecy might linger. This extends beyond the digital realm to encompass every facet of life. Open the doors to hidden corners, ushering in the light of truth.

3. *Confront the Lust of the Eyes:* "

For everything in the world—the lust of the flesh, the lust of the eyes, and the pride of life—comes not from the Father but from the world. 17 The world and its desires pass away, but whoever does the will of God lives forever."

The scriptural call in 1 John 2:16-17 to confront the lust of the eyes resonates in this strategy. Expose your eyes to the world, bringing every thought captive to align with the teachings of Christ *(2 Corinthians 10:5)*. This intentional act catalyzes transformation.

4. *Confess Sins and Dump Up:* The vulnerability doesn't stop at actions but extends to the heart. Confess sins, not just to God but to your wife or a trusted friend. This act, often referred to as "dumping up," is a deliberate choice to bring hidden struggles into the light, fostering a culture of accountability and support.

Remember, this strategy isn't solely about disclosure; it's a journey toward deeper connection and a testament to the transformative power of a marriage founded on openness and trust. Through the strength derived from Christ, this strategy emerges as a powerful means to fortify marital bonds and navigate the challenges of life hand in hand.

Strategy#6: Stare at Your Wife or Husband

Moving on to our sixth strategy, a simple yet impactful practice—staring at your spouse. Under the guidance of the Holy Spirit, this strategy appears as a deliberate act to imprint the image of your spouse deeply into your mind, birthing remarkable outcomes.

Key Components of Strategy #6

1. *Divine Imprinting:* The Holy Spirit's directive to burn the image of your spouse into your mind sets the stage for revolution. This intentional act is not mere observation; it is a sacred gaze with the potential to shape perceptions and foster a deeper connection.

2. *Consistent Affirmation:* When caught in the act of gazing, respond with the first positive thought that springs to mind. Whether it is an expression of love or an acknowledgment of physical beauty, these affirmations become threads weaving the positive emotions in your marital relationship.

3. Exclusivity Warning: The humor injected into the strategy—stressing that this practice is exclusive to your spouse—serves as a lighthearted reminder of the sanctity of marital bonds. The LOL moment encapsulates the intimate nature of this strategy, emphasizing that it is not a directive for interactions outside the sacred covenant of marriage.

4. Scriptural Anchor in Matthew 6:22,23:

> **"The eye is the lamp of the body. If your eyes are healthy, your whole body will be full of light."**

The strategy finds resonance with the scriptural wisdom in Matthew 6:22,23, underlining the significance of the eyes as the lamp of the body. This scriptural anchor reinforces the transformative potential of intentional, loving gazes within the context of marriage.

This strategy invites couples to engage in a deliberate act of love, infusing their daily interactions with the beauty and positivity inherent in acknowledging and appreciating each other. The simplicity of staring becomes a canvas upon which the Holy Spirit paints a vibrant portrait of marital intimacy and connection.

Strategy #7: Be Grateful

This strategy prompts us to cultivate gratitude within the sacred space of marriage. Guided by the

Holy Spirit, it beckons couples to embrace gratitude as a foundational element for fostering joy, contentment, and an enduring connection.

Here are important aspects of this strategy:

1. *The Holy Spirit's Guidance:* At the heart of this strategy lies a reliance on the Holy Spirit's guidance. Allowing the Spirit to cultivate gratitude within, couples are encouraged to shift their focus from self-centered thoughts, paving the way for a mindset grounded in appreciation.

2. *Overcoming Misery Through Gratitude:* The strategy addresses the difficult path of self-centered thinking that often leads to misery. By consistently practicing gratitude, couples can redirect their attention from perceived lack and flaws to the abundance of blessings, both big and small.

3. *Finding Gratitude in Simplicity:* This strategy invites couples to recognize and express gratitude in seemingly mundane instances—a gentle rain while staying dry, the rhythmic beating of the heart, the presence of family, children, and pets. This simple act of thanksgiving unveils the beauty of daily life.

4. *Embracing Purpose and Surrender:* The strategy goes beyond immediate circumstances, prompting couples to acknowledge their purpose in God's plan. Through faith and surrender, the awareness of being

created for a significant role in the divine narrative becomes a wellspring of gratitude.

5.   *Endless List of Blessings:* Couples are encouraged to compile an endless list of blessings, recognizing that gratitude extends far beyond material possessions. Gratitude encompasses the intangible, the soulful, and the interconnected threads of marital life.

6.   *Personalized   Spiritual   Growth:*   The acknowledgment that these strategies offer just a glimpse into the range of possibilities underscores the personalized nature of spiritual growth. Each couple's journey is unique, and the Holy Spirit is envisioned as the divine craftsman, tailoring a bespoke plan for marital bliss.

Through this strategy, the Holy Spirit beckons couples to consciously foster an attitude of gratitude within the context of marriage. As they traverse the ebb and flow of life's moments, this strategy serves as a compass, guiding them toward a deeper appreciation for each other.

Strategy#8: Accept Corrections

In the exploration of the eighth strategy, a pivotal principle takes center stage—the willingness to accept correction within the context of a faith-filled relationship. Anchored in humility and a recognition of the unique journey each person undertakes, this strategy encourages couples to view corrections as valuable opportunities for mutual growth.

This approach emphasizes cultivating a mindset shift, urging couples to recognize that corrections and rebukes from a spouse or a faith-filled friend stem from genuine concern. Rather than viewing correction as a sign of weakness, it is a portal for learning and growth.

True humility is defined in this strategy, clarifying that it does not involve weakness or accepting mistreatment. Instead, it invites couples to approach situations with openness, acknowledging that both partners are on a journey of continuous learning and refinement.

Drawing a parallel between unique fingerprints and the personalized plan crafted by the Holy Spirit, the strategy highlights the individuality of each person's spiritual journey. The Holy Spirit's plan is envisioned as elaborate, considering one's character, experiences, strengths, and challenges.

Couples are encouraged to place trust in the Lord, recognizing that the Holy Spirit intimately understands their innermost being. This trust forms the foundation for a transformative process tailored to shape and elevate their spiritual walks in alignment with their individuality.

The strategy underscores the simplicity of salvation in embracing spiritual, emotional, and physical deliverance through the name of Jesus.

By wholeheartedly adopting His teachings, couples could walk on a transformative journey leading to profound liberation and spiritual fulfillment.

This method emphasizes that the journey toward spiritual freedom is unique for each individual. Guided by the wisdom and grace found in the name of Jesus, couples are invited to embrace the unparalleled depth of this journey, understanding that it extends to every facet of life.

This strategy extends an invitation to couples—an invitation to approach correction with openness, viewing them as stepping stones for growth. As they navigate this strategy, couples find themselves on a life-changing journey, preciously designed by the hands of the Holy Spirit, toward true freedom in Christ.

Strategy #9: Respect

In marriage, it's crucial never to belittle your spouse, whether in your thoughts, in private conversations, or in public settings. Such behavior does not befit a lifelong commitment. Instead, strive to uplift and support your spouse, recognizing that your words and actions can deeply impact the strength and joyfulness of your relationship.

Expanding on this concept, it's essential to understand the power of words and attitudes in a marriage.

When you constantly criticize or belittle your spouse, even if only in your thoughts, it creates a negative atmosphere that can erode the foundation of your relationship.

In private, disagreements and conflicts are inevitable in any relationship, but how you address them matters. Instead of resorting to insults or put-downs, strive for open, honest communication that focuses on finding solutions and understanding each other's perspectives.

In public, it's even more critical to show respect and support for your spouse. Criticizing or making fun of them in front of others can be deeply hurtful and damaging to your relationship.

It's important to present a united front and address any issues privately, maintaining a sense of dignity and respect for each other in all situations.

By choosing to uplift and encourage your spouse, you not only strengthen your bond but also create a loving and respectful environment that nurtures a lifetime relationship.

SUMMARY:

In my journey toward a godly marriage and relationships, 2 Corinthians 10:4 serves as a guiding principle, emphasizing the divine power that transcends worldly weapons. The Holy Spirit imparted transformative strategies through visions, images, and verses, steering me toward a fulfilling marriage.

A second vision revealed a dull diamond, representing how I treated my wife. In response, the Holy Spirit guided me to polish away life's stains daily, addressing the hurt I inflicted. Another revelation emphasized maintaining eye contact and avoiding the lustful gaze of the past.

These strategies, guided by the Holy Spirit, highlighted the profound impact of love, honor, and cherish in marriage. Recognizing vows as sacred, I delved into their meanings.

- **Strategy #1:** Love, based on 1 Corinthians 13:4-8, emphasizes patience, kindness, and enduring love. Memorizing and placing these virtues prominently fosters daily practice.

- **Strategy #2:** Honor involves emulating Christ's active love, cleansing, and presenting spouses blameless. It calls for refraining from actions that dishonor, aligning with selfless love.

- **Strategy #3:** Cherish, drawn from Ephesians 5:29, emphasizes caring for spouses physically and emotionally. Fixing thoughts on one's spouse creates a protective boundary, fostering deepened love.

- **Strategy #4:** Laying down one's life aligns with Luke 9:23 and Matthew 10:39, emphasizing selfless service and surrendering to find joy and fulfillment.

- **Strategy #5:** Bringing to light, inspired by Philippians 4:13, involves transparency, giving spouses access, and confessing sins for accountability.

- **Strategy #6:** Staring at one's spouse, as guided by the Holy Spirit, imprints the image on the heart, fostering a protective love.

- **Strategy #7:** Gratitude, cultivated in every situation, counters self-centeredness, fostering a constant sense of thankfulness.

- **Strategy #8:** Accepting correction recognizes the uniqueness of spiritual journeys, promoting openness to learn and grow.

- **Strategy #9:** Never cut your spouse down in your mind, in private and in public. It is not fitting for someone to cut anyone down if you intend to stay with them for the rest of your life.

These strategies, individually tailored by the Holy Spirit, offer a holistic approach to godly relationships, fostering love, transparency, humility, and gratitude. The journey is unique to each individual, guided by the wisdom and grace found in Christ's teachings.

The lyrics of this song, "The Greatest Feeling," describe the greatest feeling: the profound forgiveness of the Father and my wife's love that is beyond compare. Take your phone and scan the QR code to listen to the song on YouTube.

The Greatest Feeling

Chapter 14: The Conclusion of the Matter

Ecclesiastes 12:14

Now all has been heard; this is the conclusion of the matter: Fear God and keep His commandments, for this is the duty of all mankind.

Ecclesiastes 12:14 encapsulates the book's concluding wisdom and essence. The author, traditionally believed to be King Solomon, reflects on the myriad experiences and pursuits detailed earlier in the book. Having explored the futility of many worldly endeavors, the verse presents a concise and profound conclusion. All that has been heard implies that the various perspectives, musings, and observations about life have been considered and examined thoroughly.

After this thorough exploration, the verse distills the wisdom into a succinct imperative: Fear God and keep his commandments, for this is the duty of all mankind.

1. Fear God: This phrase doesn't imply terror but a deep reverence and awe for the divine. It suggests acknowledging God's sovereignty, wisdom, and authority in one's life.

2. Keep His commandments: This emphasizes the importance of living by the moral and ethical guidelines set forth by God. It suggests obedience to

God's will as expressed through His teachings and moral principles.

3. Duty of all mankind: The verse underscores that this reverence for God and adherence to His commandments is not specific to a particular group or community but is a universal obligation for all humanity.

In essence, the verse is a call to prioritize spiritual and moral values in life. It suggests that true fulfillment and purpose are found in a life grounded in the fear of God and holding fast to His commandments.

The duty of all mankind, according to this verse, lies in recognizing the divine, living in harmony with His principles, and finding meaning beyond the fleeting pursuits of the world. It echoes a timeless message that transcends cultural and historical contexts, emphasizing the enduring significance of a life guided by reverence for the divine and adherence to moral principles.

God's Word has the answer to everything that pertains to a godly life. The more we know Him, the closer he becomes, and the more we hear His voice, the more we come to understand

His message. He created you for a great purpose. Let's live in it! This is what the Father thinks of you and what He calls you.

Beloved Col 3:12

Beautiful Ps 149:4

Chosen Eph 1:4

Precious Is 43:4

Safe John 5:18

Loved 1 John 4:10

Clean John 15:3

Presentable Hebrews 10:22

Protected Psalm 91:14

Welcomed Ephesians 3:12

An Heir Romans 8:17

Complete Colossians 2:10

Holy Hebrews 10:10

Forgiven Psalms 103:3

Adopted Ephesians 1:5

Your Delight Psalms 147:11

Unashamed Romans 10:11

Known Psalms 139:1

Planned Ephesians 1:11,12

Gifted 2 Timothy 1:6

Provided For Timothy 6:17

Treasured Deuteronomy 7:6

Pure 1 Corinthians 6:11

Established Romans 16:25

A work of Art Ephesians 2:10

Free from Condemnation Romans 8:1

Your Child Romans 8:15

Your friend John 15:15

A precious Bride Revelation 19:7

Knowing this, how can we not serve this wonderful God?

While we were yet sinners, Christ died for us Romans 5:8.

Let's do the same.

If this book has helped you in any way, please email me at greg@tgdahl.com

I would love to hear from you and read your story. Please be encouraged to write your own story and affect those around you. God bless you!

www.ingramcontent.com/pod-product-compliance
Lightning Source LLC
Chambersburg PA
CBHW071324150726
47997CB00002B/595